THEODORE ROOSEVELT

THEODORE ROOSEVELT

THEODORE ROOSEVELT

BY

LORD CHARNWOOD

THE ATLANTIC MONTHLY PRESS

BOSTON

TO DOCTOR WALLACE BUTTRICK

Dear Buttrick,—

If Walter Hines Page, whom we both loved, were still with us, I should have wished to dedicate this little book to him and to you jointly; as it is, I am proud of your permission to dedicate it to you. I know that he would have disagreed with much that I say in it, and very likely you will do so. But it is an attempt in the way of mutual discussion, between people of our two countries, of subjects interesting to them both; and I believe that every candid attempt of that kind contributes a little towards a cause for which our friend cared supremely, and in which he valued your counsel and commanded such small service as I could give. He was emphatically a plain American, which was why he was so much liked here, and nothing could ever have Anglicized him in the least. But he desired passionately the growth of understanding and of ready human sympathy between your people and the peoples of that strange "Commonwealth of Nations," the British Empire, seeing that you and we are trustees of a common heritage, and are so placed in the world that our concord can greatly further, our discord greatly hinder, the welfare of mankind. It is with happy memories, with high regard for your work, and with enduring affection, that I send this little essay in gratitude to you.

Always sincerely yours,

CHARNWOOD.

October 1, 1923

CONTENTS

		PAGE
	CHRONOLOGY	ix
I	BOYHOOD AND EDUCATION	3 ✓
II	BEGINNING A CAREER	18
III	NEW YORK, WASHINGTON, AND CUBA	38
IV	NINETEENTH-CENTURY AMERICA	62
V	DOMESTIC AFFAIRS DURING ROOSEVELT'S PRESIDENCY	80
VI	THE INHERITED FOREIGN POLICY	105
VII	FOREIGN ACHIEVEMENTS OF THE FIRST TERM	125
VIII	PEACEFUL TRIUMPHS OF THE SECOND TERM	146
IX	MANY ADVENTURES	159
X	THE GREAT WAR AND THE END	183
	A LETTER FROM THEODORE ROOSEVELT TO LADY DELAMERE	213
	INDEX	227

CHRONOLOGY[1]

1858 October 27. *Born at 28 East Twentieth Street, New York City.*

"My father was the best man I ever knew. My mother was a sweet, gracious, beautiful Southern woman, a delightful companion and beloved by everybody."

1880 June 30. *Graduates from Harvard University.*

"The teaching which I received was genuinely democratic in one way. It was not so democratic in another. I grew into manhood thoroughly imbued with the feeling that a man must be respected for what he made of himself. But I had also, consciously or unconsciously, been taught that socially and industrially pretty much the whole duty of man lay in thus making the best of himself; that he should be honest in his dealings with others and charitable in the old-fashioned way to the unfortunate; but that it was no part of his business to join with others in trying to make things better for the many by curbing the abnormal and excessive development of individualism in a few."

October 27. *Marries Alice Hathaway Lee.*

1882 *Publishes* The Naval War of 1812.

1882–1884 *Member of the New York State Assembly.*

"I put myself in the way of things happening; and they happened" . . . "During my three years' service in the Legislature I worked on a very simple philosophy of government. It was that personal character and initiative are the prime requisites in political and social life."

---

[1]This Table has been most kindly supplied by Mr. Hermann Hagedorn, director of the Roosevelt Memorial Association.

1883   September.   *Establishes himself as a ranchman
in western Dakota.*

1884   February 14.   *Death of his mother and his wife.*

"It was a grim and an evil fate, but I have never believed
it did any good to flinch or yield for any blow, nor does
it lighten the blow to cease from working." (Private
letter, March 1884.)

April.   *As Chairman of the Committee on Cities,
presents report which results in vital changes in
the charter of New York City.*

June.   *Delegate to the Republican National Convention.*

1884–1886   *Ranchman in the Bad Lands of Dakota.*

"It was still the Wild West in those days, the Far West,
the West of Owen Wister's stories and Frederic Reming-
ton's drawings, the soldier and the cowpuncher. That
land of the West has gone now, 'gone, gone with lost
Atlantis,' gone to the isle of ghosts and of strange dead
memories. . . . In that land we led a hardy life. Ours
was the glory of work and the joy of living."

1885   *Publishes* Hunting Trips of a Ranchman.

1886   November.   *Candidate for Mayor of New York.
Defeated by Abram S. Hewitt.*

"But anyway, I had a bully time."

December 2.   *Marries Edith Kermit Carow, in
London.*

1887   *Publishes* Life of Thomas Hart Benton.

1888   *Publishes* Life of Gouverneur Morris.

     Publishes Ranch Life and the Hunting Trail.

     Publishes Essays in Practical Politics.

1889   *Publishes first two volumes of* The Winning of
the West; *succeeding volumes were published in
1894 and 1896.*

1891   *Publishes* History of New York.

1893   *Publishes* The Wilderness Hunter.

1889–1895   *United States Civil Service Commissioner.*

"The opposition to the reform is generally well led by
skilled parliamentarians, and they fight with the vin-
dictiveness natural to men who see a chance of striking
at the institution which has baffled their ferocious
greed. These men have a gift at office-mongering, just
as other men have a peculiar knack in picking pockets;
and they are joined by all the honest dull men, who vote
wrong out of pure ignorance, and by a very few sincere
and intelligent, but wholly misguided people."

1895   *Publishes, in collaboration with Henry Cabot
Lodge,* Hero Tales from American History.

1895–1897   *President of the Police Commission of the
City of New York.*

"There is nothing of the purple in it. It is as grimy as all
work for municipal reform over here must be for some

decades to come; and it is inconceivably arduous, disheartening, and irritating, beyond almost all other work of the kind. . . . It is not work to be done on a rosewater basis."

1897 *Publishes* American Ideals.

1897–1898 *Assistant Secretary of the Navy.*

"The shots that hit are the shots that count."

1898 May. *Resigns as Assistant Secretary to become Lieutenant-Colonel of the First U. S. Volunteer Cavalry (the Rough Riders).*

"A man's usefulness depends upon his living up to his ideals in so far as he can. Now, I have consistently preached what our opponents are pleased to call 'Jingo doctrines' for a good many years. One of the commonest taunts directed at men like myself is that we are armchair and parlor Jingoes who wish to see others do what we only advocate doing. I care very little for such a taunt, except as it affects my usefulness, but I cannot afford to disregard the fact that my power for good, whatever it may be, would be gone if I did n't try to live up to the doctrines I have to preach."

June 24. *Baptism of fire at Las Guasimas.*

July 1. *Battle of San Juan Hill.*

"As for the political effect of my actions — in the first place, I never can get on in politics, and in the second, I would rather have led that charge and earned my colonelcy than served three terms in the United States Senate. It makes me feel as though I could now leave something to my children which will serve as an apology for my having existed."

1898   November 8.   *Elected Governor of New York.*

"At that time boss rule was at its very zenith. . . .
In each case I did my best to persuade Mr. Platt not to
oppose me. . . . It was only after I had exhausted
all the resources of my patience that I would finally, if
he still proved obstinate, tell him that I intended to
make the fight anyhow."

1899   *Publishes* The Rough Riders.

1900   *Publishes* Oliver Cromwell.

Publishes The Strenuous Life.

June 21.   *Nominated for Vice-President by the
Republican Party.*

"If I have been put on the shelf, my enemies will find
that I can make it a cheerful place of abode."

1901   March 4.   *Takes office as Vice-President.*

September 14.   *President McKinley dies as the
result of an assassin's bullet; Roosevelt becomes
twenty-sixth President of the United States.*

"The course I followed, of regarding the Executive as
subject only to the people, and, under the Constitution, bound to serve the people affirmatively in cases
where the Constitution does not explicitly forbid him
to render the service, was substantially the course
followed by both Andrew Jackson and Abraham
Lincoln."

1902   June 17.   *Reclamation Act.*

1902   June 28.   *Isthmian Canal Act.*

October 15.   *Roosevelt settles the coal strike.*

"May Heaven preserve me from ever again dealing with
so wooden-headed a set as these coal-operators, when
I wish to preserve their interests!" . . . "I shall
never forget the mixture of relief and amusement I felt
when I thoroughly grasped the fact that while they
would heroically submit to anarchy rather than have
Tweedledum, yet if I would call it Tweedledee, they
would accept it with rapture; it gave me an illuminating glimpse into one corner of the mighty brains of
these 'captains of industry.'"

December 31.   *Roosevelt settles the Venezuela
affair.*

"I told John Hay that I would now see the German
Ambassador, Herr von Holleben, myself, and that I
intended to bring matters to an early conclusion. Our
navy was in very efficient condition."

1903   February 19.   *Elkins Rebate Act.*

March.   *Roosevelt settles the Alaskan Boundary
dispute.*

November 13.   *Recognition of the Republic of
Panama.*

"Panama declared itself independent and wanted to
complete the Panama Canal, and opened negotiations
with us. I had two courses open. I might have taken
the matter under advisement and put it before the
Senate, in which case we should have had a number
of most able speeches on the subject, and they would
have been going on now, and the Panama Canal would

be in the dim future yet. We would have had a half century of discussion, and perhaps the Panama Canal. I preferred we should have the Panama Canal first and the half century of discussion afterward."

1903   December 17.   *Reciprocity Treaty with Cuba.*

1904   November 8.   *Elected President over Alton B. Parker, the Democratic nominee.*

"I am glad to be President in my own right."

1905   March 4.   *Inaugurated as President.*

September 5.   *Signing of Russo-Japanese Treaty.*

"It is enough to give anyone a sense of sardonic amusement to see the way in which the people generally, not only in my own country but elsewhere, gauge the work purely by the fact that it succeeded. If I had not brought about peace I should have been laughed at and condemned. Now I am over-praised."

Publishes Outdoor Pastimes of an American Hunter.

1906   June 11.   *Forest Homestead Act.*

June 29.   *Hepburn Rate Act.*

June 30.   *Food and Drug Act.*

1907   December 16.   *American fleet starts round the world.*

1909   February 22.   *Return of the fleet.*

"In my own judgment the most important service that I rendered to peace was the voyage of the battle-fleet round the world."

March 4.   *Roosevelt retires from the Presidency, being succeeded by William Howard Taft.*

March 23.   *Sails for Africa.*

1909–1910   *Hunting in Central Africa.*

"There are no words that can tell the hidden spirit of the wilderness, that can reveal its mystery, its melancholy, and its charm. There is delight in the hardy life of the open, in long rides, rifle in hand, in the thrill of the fight with dangerous game. Apart from this, yet mingled with it, is the strong attraction of the silent places, of the large tropic moons, and the splendor of the new stars; where the wanderer sees the awful glory of sunrise and sunset in the wide waste spaces of the earth, unworn of man, and changed only by the slow change of the ages through time everlasting."

1910   March 14.   *Arrives at Khartum.*

May 31.   *Address at the Guildhall, London.*

"Either you have the right to be in Egypt or you have not, either it is or it is not your duty to establish and keep order. . . . Some nation must govern Egypt. I hope and believe that you will decide that it is your duty to be that nation."

June 18.   *Returns to New York.*

Publishes African Game Trails.

1910   *Publishes* The New Nationalism.

1912   February 25.   *Announces candidacy for the Republican nomination for President.*

"My hat is in the ring."

Publishes Realizable Ideals.

June.   *Defeated at the Republican National Convention.*

August 7.   *Nominated for President by the Progressive Party.*

"This country will not be a good place for any of us to live in if it is not a reasonably good place for all of us to live in." . . . "Laws are enacted for the benefit of the whole people, and cannot and must not be construed as permitting discrimination against some of the people."

October 14.   *Shot at Milwaukee.*

"I did not care a rap for being shot. It is a trade risk, which every prominent public man ought to accept as a matter of course."

November 5.   *Defeated by Woodrow Wilson.*

1913   *Publishes* Theodore Roosevelt — an Autobiography.

Publishes History as Literature and Other Essays.

1914–1915 Winter. *In the Brazilian wilderness; explores the River of Doubt.*

"I had to go. It was my last chance to be a boy."

1914 *Publishes* Through the Brazilian Wilderness.

Publishes, in collaboration with Edmund Heller, Life Histories of African Game Animals.

1915 January 1. *Publishes* America and the World War.

"The kind of 'neutrality' which seeks to preserve 'peace' by timidly refusing to live up to our plighted word and to denounce and take action against such wrong as that committed in the case of Belgium, is unworthy of an honorable and powerful people. Dante reserved a special place of infamy in the Inferno for those base angels who dared side neither with evil nor with good. Peace is ardently to be desired, but only as the handmaid of righteousness. The only peace of permanent value is the peace of righteousness. There can be no such peace until well-behaved, highly civilized small nations are protected from oppression and subjugation."

May. *Libel-suit, William Barnes vs. Theodore Roosevelt; decided in favor of Roosevelt.*

1916 *Publishes* A Booklover's Holidays in the Open.

Publishes Fear God and Take Your Own Part.

June. *Nominated for President by the Progressive Party; refuses the nomination and gives his support to the Republican candidate, Charles E. Hughes.*

"We have room for but one loyalty, loyalty to the United States. We have room for but one language, the language of the Declaration of Independence and the Gettysburg speech."

1917   February.   *Requests permission of President Wilson to raise and equip a division of volunteers for service in France.*

"Peace is not the end. Righteousness is the end." . . . "If I must choose between righteousness and peace I choose righteousness."

May.   *Request finally refused.*

Publishes The Foes of Our Own Household.

1918   July.   *Death of Quentin Roosevelt in France. Roosevelt refuses Republican nomination for Governor of New York.*

Publishes The Great Adventure.

"Our present business is to fight, and to continue fighting until Germany is brought to her knees. Our next business will be to help guarantee the peace of justice for the world at large, and to set in order the affairs of our own household."

1919   January 6.   *Death of Roosevelt.*

"All of us who give service, and stand ready for sacrifice, are the torch-bearers. We run with the torches until we fall, content if we can then pass them to the hands of other runners. . . . Both life and death are parts of the same Great Adventure.''

[The quotations above are taken in the main from *Theodore Roosevelt and His Time*, *African Game Trails*, *Theodore Roosevelt — an Autobiography*, *The Great Adventure* (Charles Scribner's Sons); *American Ideals* (G. P. Putnam's Sons); and *The Boys' Life of Theodore Roosevelt* (Harper and Brothers).]

THEODORE ROOSEVELT

THEODORE ROOSEVELT

I

BOYHOOD AND EDUCATION

THIS fugitive study of a memorable life may at several points help to make clearer issues which are momentous still. If it is written with no desire to give offense, but no obsequious fear of doing so, it may contribute to frank and sympathetic discussion between two great peoples. Above all, it may arouse more interest in a powerful and a noble man, whose fate it was for a considerable while to rivet and indeed fatigue the attention of civilized mankind, then to undergo eclipse, which outside his own country endured; and it may do this last while the recognition of greatness in the modern world continues to be peculiarly needed. It can claim to do no more. Candidly my reason for writing it is, that, having been invited to do so, I am disabled from refusing by a boyish hero-worship which I conceived very long ago for Theodore Roosevelt — then and ever since unknown to me.

When a statesman has been only four years dead, the disadvantages of a biographer who belongs to another country are almost unmixed,

though, after a longer time, he would on the whole
be in a position of advantage. Besides this, the existing books on the subject of this biographical
essay are not a few; they cover their ground very
adequately; and several of them are extraordinarily
good books. But in England, at any rate, they
have been almost unnoticed in comparison with
any comparable memoirs. It is strange to me that
I seldom hear mention of a political biography such
as Mr. Bishop's *Life and Times of Theodore Roosevelt*,
told, as it is, chiefly by an admirably restrained
selection from the letters of a first-rate letter-writer,
and ranging, as it does in the charming correspondence between Roosevelt and Sir George Trevelyan,
so far beyond the regions of mere politics. Nor can
I here help adding the titles of Mr. Thayer's brief
and wise *Theodore Roosevelt, an Intimate Biography*,
of Mr. Hermann Hagedorn's poetic but truthful
study of a vanished frontier life in his *Roosevelt in
the Bad Lands*, and of Roosevelt's own *Autobiography*.
I shall be well content to write even a very slight
book if it serves to advertise its predecessors.

Theodore Roosevelt was born in New York, on
October 27, 1858. Of his ancestors, concerning
whom he himself recounted shortly and humorously
the little that was worth saying, we need note only
that they represented many nations, and chiefly the

robustly Protestant elements in those nations. Like
his name, the dominant tradition of his family past
was Dutch; but the Dutch blood was blended with
that of French Huguenots, German Protestants of
the Rhineland who fled from Louis XIV, Scotsmen
from the confines of the Highlands, Ulstermen,
Southern Irishmen, Welsh Quakers; there was also
a little English blood coming partly through the
Pennsylvanian Quakers, and partly by way of Hol-
land. How the potent but incalculable effects of
physiological inheritance show themselves in any
individual is a matter of most idle speculation, but
a man's own idea about his ancestry is important
and not always harmful. The whole history of
Roosevelt's native city illustrates the composite
character of the American population even from
early days, and his own pedigree was a marked
instance of it. His writings insist much on this
composite character and even exaggerate it.

Americans who understand and value England
are often conscious of an Anglo-Saxon stock from
which they come, and to which, and to its central
home in this island, they owe and pay a certain
loyalty. Now few Americans have understood
England so well as Roosevelt; no Americans and
few Englishmen have understood the British Empire as he did; and very few men have ever had so

many, such well-chosen, or such dearly cherished friendships with men of another land as he had with Englishmen. But from first to last he had no Anglo-Saxon feeling. The notion of an exclusive friendship between the English-speaking peoples would not have appealed to him. In theory he would have been as ready to find quarrel with England as with any country. He had in the end good reason to fall foul of the hybrid American citizenship which retained an active allegiance to Germany or to Ireland; but his sentiment was outraged hardly less by those tendencies of culture, or more often of fashion and of pleasure-seeking, which may lead an American to feel or to wish himself an Englishman. Hence in later years that insistence upon an "Americanism," which might seem either meaningless or blatant to men of other countries whose patriotism is not exposed to these subtle dangers. It was on the basis of an exceeding respect and love for the native tradition of his own country, with its motley racial origins, that he reared an unusual capacity for fair and respectful dealing with other countries, and a still more unusual love of individual human worth, not only in many different forms but in widely separated lands.

He was preëminently American in another sense. Like Lincoln, of whom, with a humbler estimate of himself than might be supposed, he aspired to be the disciple, he was no more a Northerner than a Southerner. His father, after whom he was called Theodore, and whom he venerated but did not (it would seem) resemble, was a reasonably prosperous business man, attentive to his affairs, but untiring, original, and sagacious in every sound work of philanthropy; with a redeeming love for dancing and a dash of reckless courage in him; a punctual but inaustere adherent of his Church, and possessed of a rare faculty of companionship with his children. When the Civil War came, his whole heart was in the cause of the North, and he was a man of fighting spirit; but his wife came of a prominent family in Georgia, and her nearest relations were in arms for the South. A sound feeling led him, therefore, to find his way of serving the Union in distinguished and able services, not exempt from toil or from danger, to the wounded. The younger Theodore's memory began with a time when the war was at its height, and when he was already a passionate little Unionist who, in saying his prayers at his mother's knee, once got back his own, after some rebuke from her, by invoking a blessing on the Northern arms. That beloved mother was never in her political opinions reconciled or "reconstructed," and in no other sense needed to be reconciled. The nursery culture of Theodore and his brother and sisters was enriched with the genial folklore of the plantation. Two uncles of his served in the Southern Navy, one of them designed that ill-omened ship, the Alabama; the other fired her last gun. They lived to become in England somewhat virulent British Tories, but never to cherish bitterness against their victorious kinsfolk. Their famous nephew was reared in a Unionism which went deeper than a mere assertion of supremacy, in a home atmosphere charged with political difference which must be sternly fought out, but which never raised a malicious thought.

In strange contrast with his adult life, his childhood was dominated by physical suffering and weakness, caused by asthma. He was an object for special home care and never went to school. It is common enough for a delicate child to end with a rather sudden change into an unusually vigorous man or woman. But the change was promoted in his case by deliberate physical culture, provoked in part by the discovery of his helplessness in an encounter with boys who teased him, and encouraged by the teaching of his father, that for him it was a duty to "make his own body." It will be needless to recur often in these pages to the physical prowess which he ultimately achieved. His bodily growth was slow; but, helped by this effort at self-development and by his whole way of life in early manhood, it resulted in a very exceptional robustness of frame. He had the drawback of very short sight and had to wear glasses whenever they could be worn. "I had no idea," he remarks, "how beautiful the world was till I got those spectacles." It is curious how many people who have shared this great disadvantage with him have been like him in the power of rapid and delicate observation. In riding, shooting, boxing, and not a few other things which demand strength, or skill, or nerve, or all three, he rose to a very fair degree of excellence; he was fond of declaring that most men could do as well as he in all these things if they tried, while in each of them a small minority could become first-rate, and in each a small minority was naturally hopeless.

It would be doing him an injustice to say that he pursued his various sports upon principle; his love of them was part of a general sense of the whole joy of life, a joy from which the men who shrank would shrink from life's duty as well. But deliberately he thought it admirable to make one's body a good servant, and deliberately he valued the moral discipline of those ways in which, without criminal recklessness, the danger of death now and then becomes perceptible to a man and he feels himself dependent for his safety on his own best efforts. He learned a sympathy which is often lacking in men of books, such as he was, for all manner of rough "men of their hands." Perhaps without his early experience of weakness and suffering he could never have learned to link so intimately as he did all the delights of exubèrant vitality with the most serious of human purposes. When in later years the robustious ex-President testified to English undergraduates of Cambridge against the sin of mere athleticism, he had recently, while at the White House, had the sight of one eye knocked out in boxing; and he continued to addict himself to the like pursuits, just so far as age allowed him; but he was none the less giving utterance to a conviction in which he lived.

In another way, closely connected with this, his early sheltered home life, with parents who took due care that their children should have country pleasures, gave scope for a ruling taste of his which school life, for all its advantages, sometimes represses. He became of himself an eager naturalist — the sort of boy who is likely at any time to have a toad in his pocket — and founded with his sisters, in the nursery, "the Roosevelt Museum." This impulse, too, lasted to the end. The "charm of birds," the romance which attaches to beasts, great and little, and their haunts, the beauty of nature in its broadest and in its minuter aspects — to these he would turn back whenever he could; and that truthfulness of observation which goes with genuine love of them inspired some of the best written pages of his vigorous and profuse literary work.

Perhaps, too, the instincts of the traveler, and the readiness to know and like far lands and alien breeds of men, were fostered by early training. For the children were taken abroad early. Their first trip to Europe, when Theodore was ten, was indeed a failure educationally. They all hated it; the works of art which were to have been a revelation to their little souls bored them, and there is no indication that he ever became very much awake to beauty of that order. But four years afterwards they traveled in the Holy Land and Egypt, going far up the Nile, with which he was to be well acquainted later. Ancient monuments could be tolerated and even enjoyed now, for Theodore had his first gun and could begin his career as a collector of birds. On the way back they passed a summer with a German family in Dresden, and the boy acquired an affection which never forsook him for the qualities which, in quiet times, are most conspicuous in ordinary German life.

As the boy grew older and less delicate, boating

and fishing and shooting adventures played a larger part in his life, and the keen eye of Theodore's mother began to see a strain of the Berserker in his character, for which he seems to have been wholesomely chaffed. All the while, not to speak of the tuition which supplied the lack of schooling, he was getting that broader education which is peculiar to homes where good books are put in young people's way but never forced upon them, and where the best of them are enjoyed amid hearty fun by the children and their parents in common, without a suspicion in their minds that they are, as in fact this family was, an uncommonly "cultivated" lot.

Further details of Roosevelt's early days do not concern us. His autobiography treats of them in a pleasant and a sensible fashion, and, here as throughout, the more expansive record of his life by his sister, Mrs. Douglas Robinson, is not lacking in humor or in affectionate charm. But it does concern us to notice that he passed the remainder of his life in accordance with this beginning. The, possibly audacious, publication since his death of his letters to his own children, has given us an image of his later days which recalls in full that which we possess of his father's and mother's household. His years held plenty of wandering, adventure, and turmoil, and were passed, even excessively, under the public eye; yet there can seldom have been even a moderately stirring man more firmly anchored to home and all its relationships, and to whom, for all his stirrings and ambitions, the quiet central things of life counted more. And his was a life highly favored. There was a brief interval of loneliness and sorrow, and the element of tragedy which marks the career of most great actors in public affairs stands out strongly enough in his; but there was given to him full measure of that intensest happiness upon which biography does well to touch only with the light hand of reverence.

We need linger even less over the four years at Harvard, with which the sheltered days of a life that never sought again any shelter, closed. Delightful as college life normally is, both to live and to look at, the dreariness of tattling reminiscence about it is usually proportionate to that delight. We may take it as certain that Roosevelt loved such a place as Harvard and that it did him good; but with his purely home training and with considerable arrears of growth still to make up, he was not likely to distinguish himself much. He did not; nor was he very distinctly aware afterwards of what he had learned there. He did well in natural science and moderately well in other parts of the miscellaneously assorted curriculum which he was allowed or encouraged to choose for his college course. Quite outside that course, and unhelped by the criticism of his teachers, he began his first published book, on the Naval History of the War of 1812. Englishmen, accustomed to the more democratic life of their own universities, may be allowed to be a little shocked when they learn that his family antecedents helped him into clubs which enjoyed high social prestige. But it was not as a fashionable youth that he was noticed. The contemporaries who liked him best recall him as a shy, though agreeably pugnacious eccentric, who persisted, in spite of protest, in wearing whiskers when fashion among gilded youth had discarded them, but in other respects went his way inconspicuously. They had the insight to wonder where his own curious way would lead him, but did not guess that it would lead him to fame. In Mr. Thayer's happy phrase, the chief thing about him was "his loyalty to his own hobbies."

For some inscrutable reason it is hard to write about the combination of a fine muscular system not only with adequate animal courage but with unusually clean and lofty aims in life, without causing derision and even persuading men who are deficient in any of these respects of some occult superiority on their own part. I shall be silent therefore about more than one incident from this time onward which showed Roosevelt as the violent champion of gentle things against that which is cruel or foul. But one little edifying anecdote of his college days should be recounted since it was ominous of his fate. While at Harvard he taught in a Sunday School. He was always loyal to the spirit of his father's piety, though perhaps he never much appreciated any of its doctrines. But his first connection with a Sunday School ended in sad conflict with the denomination concerned. For there came to his class one day a little boy with a black eye; he inquired about that black eye; the little boy had honorably earned it in fighting a boy who pinched his sister; and Roosevelt commended and rewarded him. This was too much for the elders of that Church. We all know that principle of old-fashioned piety and new-fashioned enlightenment, upon which to punch another boy's head is deemed the typical exhibition of the brute in man, while the spirit of the Gospel is held to show itself in not caring how much he pinches one's sister. Against this bastard Christianity Roosevelt was destined, all his life, to do battle, and to die with the battle going against him.

Shortly before the end of his time at Harvard the

death of his father left him to his own guidance. That father had already told him that he had earned enough for his son to be free of business or a profession, if he would keep free also of expensive pleasures; he had told him, too, that he would countenance his son's taking up some nonremunerative line of work, if, though his living did not depend upon it, he "intended to do the very best work that was in him." Theodore's hope at first was to find work as a field naturalist for some scientific institution. The careers of men like Audubon fascinated him, and he continued to believe long after that there was as much value in the study of beasts as they lived, and the bigger the beast the better, as in microscopic examination, say, of infusoria in a laboratory. But the scientific authorities of Harvard discouraged him — he insisted later that theirs was a narrow view of biology, and we can at least believe that Darwin would have found a ready use for him. So the question what he should do with himself became a very doubtful one, till at last a friend who asked him about it received the startling answer: "I am going to try to help the cause of better government in New York; I don't know exactly how." His own later judgment sought candidly to belittle the Quixotic exaltation of this resolve, but his reading of his own past, if correct, only tempers its nobility with a genial boyishness. Government, he was told, was a dirty trade, in which gentlemen were not welcome and from which gentlemen should stand aloof. But, gentleman as he might be, he was nominally a citizen of a self-governing country. He did not say in his heart that as a better man he could make the world better, but he "intended to be one of the governing class" and to find out "whether he really was too weak to hold his own in the rough-and-tumble."

II

BEGINNING A CAREER

In the twenty-one years which now followed, Theodore Roosevelt did brilliant service for short periods in five very different fields of public work; this inconsecutive official experience was alternated and blended with adventure in frontier life and in war; not to speak of occasional visits to Europe or of the vast range of reading and the vigorous variety of writing which accompanied the whole. Any one of the episodes into which the story could be broken would be found full of lively incident, of brief but thoroughgoing occupation with grave matters, or of both. But we had better pass those years in rapid survey, viewing them in connection with what was to come.

Shortly after he left college, he married a Massachusetts lady, Miss Alice Hathaway Lee, who became the mother of his eldest daughter, Mrs. Longworth, but whose life partnership with him was not to last long. The young couple settled in New York. Entrance into New York politics might not prove easy, and for precaution's sake Roosevelt began studying law. Long after, during his short Vice-Presidency, he again contemplated returning to the law, but he had an evident repulsion from the requirement of taking a side regardless of one's sympathies, and the frequent further requirement of exclusive attention to the least important aspects of the matter concerned, which is incident to that august profession. For good and for ill he was unlikely to develop a great legal intellect, though, as he later reflected, an American lawyer might do a great work "for justice against legalism." Quite reasonably he felt no trouble about the broad choice of a side in politics. Historically the Republican Party stood for the Union; in root principle, so far as a distinction could be drawn, it stood for a strong national government; in its composition it included most of the leaders of industrial and commercial advance. Like most young men of his upbringing he had learned to think of that advance as in the main representing human progress, though his troubles as to the exact qualifications which this broad statement requires were to begin before long. So he took the first necessary steps to becoming a Republican politician.

The famous political machine of America had its origin in a more or less sincere zeal that the people at large should control its own government. That zeal had miscarried and long before this time, in New York City, the organization in each district formed a kind of social and political club for which a man had to be regularly proposed and elected. Into the Twenty-first District Republican Association of that city he, nevertheless, gained admission; regularly attended the meetings in a club-room, which, if otherwise dingy, was at least well furnished with spittoons; unobtrusively took stock of his queer new associates; and was received on the whole with affability, and even friendliness, though he outraged the principles of most of them by voting, with a handful of others, for "a non-partisan method of street-cleaning." Suddenly a remarkable fighting Irishman among them, Joseph Murray, for whom Roosevelt had conceived a liking without suspecting that it was returned, had an inspiration to annoy the great chief of the Club by getting Roosevelt adopted as the Republican candidate in that district for the Assembly (the lower House of the Legislature) of the State. He succeeded; the great chief took his reverse in good part, and the two practised hands together led Roosevelt around to canvass the local saloon-keepers. At the first saloon which they visited they had cause for dismay; for their candidate, being told by the saloon-keeper, who was a man of influence, that the tax on licences was too high,

answered that he should try to get it made higher.
In the rest of that canvass the candidate himself
was left at home. But he was elected to the
Assembly for the year 1882, and, largely as he
believed because Joe Murray did not find him, like
other men, so puffed up by this honor as to become
less friendly to ordinary folk, he was elected again
for the two following years.

In the Assembly at Albany "young Mr. Roosevelt
of New York, a blond young man with eyeglasses,
English side-whiskers, and a Dundreary drawl in
his speech," soon found things to fight for, made
a mark, and made some friends — of course enemies
also. He declares that he got a little bit above himself and nearly lost the position which he had won.
If so, he recovered himself quickly, and in his
third term narrowly missed being made Speaker,
becoming, instead, chairman of important committees dealing mainly with the affairs of New
York City. The great State of New York includes,
besides the famous city at its extreme southeastern
corner, from which it takes its name, other cities
far away, distinguished by industry, invention, and
public spirit; and the vast and beautiful region
which lies between them is the home of an independent farming people of no slight attractiveness
and worth. Nevertheless, for reasons over which

we need not pause here, it has not produced an illustrious Legislature. Great and rapid material development was and continues to be in progress, and so a very large proportion of the business of the Legislature consists in what in England is called Private Bill Legislation. The organization and procedure of American legislatures seem unfavorable to the fair and aboveboard transaction of such business. Unscrupulous business corporations were accustomed to buy favor not only by subscriptions to one or both of the rival party-machines, but by the direct bribery of a certain number of specially hardened and skillful legislators.

On the other hand, corporations whether unscrupulous or not were exposed to blackmail upon the part of the same expert gentry. In the milder form of jobbery, which consists in the abuse of patronage, the old hands of the opposed parties had a common interest, for the sake of which they did ingenious "deals" with each other behind the back of the Legislature at large. Public opinion could manage to remain partly ignorant, partly indifferent about it all. It was not in itself a great matter that a city of colossal wealth did not draw all the taxation that it might from a certain railway, or that the fares on the same railway were a little too low or too high; and, though the transaction through which some such minor evil arose might really be a very black business, the facts of the matter would generally be hard to discover, and to the ordinary citizen (as to the present historian) dull and unintelligible when told.

Hence in this part of his pilgrimage Roosevelt's efforts were in large part spent in discovering and defeating, or at least exposing, jobs. His first speech was a blunt statement of the case, which explained, and thus destroyed, some "deal" of a customary and plausible kind, but with undeserved profits for somebody at the back of it, between his own party, who were in a minority by only one, and the most orthodox and pestilential group in the divided Democratic majority. Soon after he faced the unpleasant task of demanding investigation into charges of venal favor to rich corporations, made against a Judge of the Supreme Court of the State. The investigation came to nothing, for some reason which was not generally assumed to lie in the uprightness of that Judge; but investigation is discouraging to corruption. When a bill, already alluded to, which would have freed the New York Elevated Railway from half its proper taxation, came around, he failed to defeat it in the Assembly, but aroused a public opinion which encouraged the Governor to veto it. And so forth.

But before the three years were out, he had more positive results to show. As the result of several fights successful and unsuccessful for bills for the better government of New York City, or against bills for its even worse government, he achieved some important steps toward reforming the constitution of that amazing municipality. He accomplished, too, a real measure of Civil Service Reform for all the larger cities in the State. He made good his old promise to the saloon-keeper, that he would advocate a heavier tax on his licence, but his proposal was defeated. More important still, he took up the demand of the Cigar-makers Trade-Union for a law to stop their trade from being carried on under foul conditions in tenement houses. Here he succeeded with the Legislature, but the Courts and the Constitution were against him — a fact with consequences in his mental history.

But the details of these struggles cannot interest us now in comparison with the mere fact that a youth, with only Harvard and a cultured home behind him, was able almost at once to become a leader and a standard-bearer in that queer legislative House. The secret of this fact, apart from his obvious moral courage, lay in a quality which is even more uncommon. He went into what his normal associates thought a very dingy crowd without the least sense of personal superiority in virtue; he was ready to fight any man or every man if real cause arose, but still more ready to be friends when friendship was possible; above all, for whatever good he did, his own heart gave the greatest praise to comrades whose scope in life was narrower than his, who could win no such praise as he won, and in some cases were knowingly inviting a vengeance which could not touch him. Anyone who is interested in politics from what he deems a high moral standpoint might do well to turn to the passages in Roosevelt's "Autobiography" which tell of Mike Costello or, still more, of Peter Kelly, or, in a different connection, of some of his prize-fighter friends, or of heroes among the police of New York. Not that there is anything very thrilling or picturesque about them, but because, in these days even more than ever, little good can be done for the mass of mankind by the most enlightened and highminded if they cannot make man-to-man friendships without elegant "respect of persons."

It went along with his essentially kindly attitude that, since he had sometimes to hit, he held "that the unforgivable crime is soft hitting." When he saw a thief, he expressed his estimate of that man's moral worth in words and tones intended to electrify the honest people who, from timidity, depraved custom, or convenient blindness, "consented unto him." Thus "the exquisite Mr. Roosevelt," as in 1882 plausible satire could still call him, developed — and had to do so — a style of oratory which the plausible satire of later days could describe with very different adjectives. And perhaps there were other reasons, too, why he came quite honestly by a superfluously forcible manner. He first spoke in earnest in a place where sometimes — of course by no means always — his words, if they were to be worth speaking, must be of the sledgehammer sort. But, as his college-mates describe him, he started not only with a full share of natural shyness — as do many forcible men — but likewise with a difficulty in clear enunciation; what was burning in him, if it was to come out at all, must come out with a rush, perhaps a roar.

If he learned some large sympathies in his legislative days, he also began to form some antipathies. His disgust was not reserved for the poorer and dirtier agents of a system in which mild corruption spread far and gross corruption did not surprise. More than one of his kindly elders, of high repute in good society, gave him well-meant counsels of wisdom which shocked him. Thus he early became alive to the sort of surreptitious connections between the world of great industrial enterprises and the

world of politics, about which he long after grew
fierce. And, what is quite a different matter, he
learned that even upright courts of justice may be
led to obstruct social progress. Mention has already
been made of his Act concerning the manufacture
of cigars in tenement houses. When he proposed
and carried this measure, he had himself pene-
trated into the unsavory dens in New York where
this manufacture destroyed whatever healthy conditions remained possible to the crowded immigrants with several families in one room. Therefore it left a deep impression on him when the courts
held that the Act was invalid, as a violation of
rights of property which the Constitution guaranteed. The principle of the decision was one which
held up for many years, in New York, reforms which
were even more needed there than in London, and
to the need of which English opinion became about
that time keenly alive. The well-meaning jurist
who delivered the decision heightened its effect
upon Roosevelt by indulging in sentimentality upon
a subject of which he knew nothing; speaking of the
lairs in which the hapless aliens concerned were
condemned to stink, he talked of "home and its
hallowed associations." Roosevelt's later policy
was not always referable to thought-out principle,
but the connecting strain of loyalty, to deep and

sincere impressions beginning far back, is generally
pretty easy to see.

This brave first flight of his in the politics of
New York State closed with an incident which disappointed some who had been readiest to admire
him, and gave the first start to whatever was honest
in a sort of censure which waited upon him ever
after. A few plain words must be said upon it.
He was sent as a delegate to the Republican National
Convention in the spring of 1884. On that memorable occasion the candidate nominated for the Presidency was James G. Blaine. Mr. Blaine was the
most brilliant and popular man of his party, but
there were grave charges against his probity. The
verdict of Mr. Rhodes on these charges is that "he
had *probably* prostituted his position as Speaker of
the House for the purpose of making money," and
Mr. Rhodes is perhaps the justest man who ever
wrote history. On the other hand, it seems sure
enough that the vast majority of rank-and-file
Republicans believed that Blaine had cleared himself. Here it may be worth while for some English
readers to notice that a man whose strict financial
honor could be doubted at all had never before
been put up as a Presidential candidate, and that the
all but inevitable effect was to break the long dom-
ination of the Republican party and secure the elec-

tion of a Democrat — that great President, Grover
Cleveland. It was the occasion when the famous
"Mugwumps" revolted from the Republican party.

Roosevelt's efforts to prevent Mr. Blaine's nomination had been conspicuous and bold. But when
the Convention had given its decision, he gave
enough active support to the chosen candidate to
mark himself as a committed party man. It was
natural that the Democratic press should denounce
him as a "reform fraud" found out; and it was
honorable in his courageous "Mugwump" friends
to be bitterly grieved. He had not acted without
grave searchings of heart. He reflected upon the
relative utility of acting "without and within the
party"; a man "could not possibly do both";
but he had once, with his eyes open, gone into
things as a party man and would continue in his
course, feeling deeply that he was "alienating
many friends and the only kind of political support
he valued." The decisive consideration for him
was, he declared, this: he had been sent as a delegate to that Convention by men who trusted him
to vote as he saw fit, but trusted him, all the same,
to abide by the vote of the majority; if he were
not to support Blaine now he should never have
accepted the position in which he had been able
to offer him a very serious opposition. At a more

memorable crisis of his life, in the Republican Convention of twenty-eight years later, we shall have to ask whether the different circumstances justified the seeming difference of his action. But this reasoning of his in 1884 admits, if an English critic can understand the case, of no possible answer, and the suspicion cast upon his manly rectitude, though quite intelligible, was totally baseless.

Here the scene changes. It was not to be expected or desired that Roosevelt, at the age of twenty-six, with all his powers still rapidly developing and his horizon becoming vast, should hold himself bound down for long to this useful work in New York State. He had already gone hunting in the Far West, and in 1883 he had bought and stocked two cattle ranches in what is now the State of North Dakota. Starting these ranches had been a delightful adventure to him; he probably enhanced its pleasure by imagining that he was likely to see his money back; possibly he enjoyed the knowledge that his wisest relatives thought the whole proceeding mad. Visits of business or of pleasure, to his ranchmen and his cattle, were frequent enough for years after. But from the autumn of 1884 to that of 1886 his home lay among them, and it was a home with a solace which his nature needed at the time. For early in 1884 his mother had passed away, and upon the following day his young wife had died in childbirth.

The Bad Lands of Dakota had been so named by French-Canadian hunters who found that traveling through these rough plains and tortuous ravines was trying even to them. They are the product of a geological history which is, perhaps fortunately, unusual. Every great wilderness has shifting and haunting beauties, of which the Bad Lands must have their full share; but, to judge from pictures, descriptions, and geological models, the utterly fantastic and freakish shapes of hill and ravine, the general aspect of desolation, and the abundance of sticky mud would specially recommend this section of the West only to the more eccentric lovers of nature's charms. The terror and havoc of the winter of 1886 and of the following spring-floods were probably greater in a country of that nature than anywhere else in the Northwest. To Roosevelt and to many a poorer man they brought heavy loss. But the Bad Lands were attractive for cattle-ranching, first, because they were unpromising for all other purposes, and secondly, because Texas and other ranching areas had already been taken up.

To drop to minor economic considerations, — such as had actually influenced the sturdy fellows from New Brunswick whom Roosevelt found there and took as partners and who proved loyal and wise friends, — the Northern Pacific Railway would then carry one out there for nothing, but charge five cents a mile for taking one back.

A little study of the map would prepare the reader to find that the arm of the law was not strong at first in the Bad Lands. Around the point where the Northern Pacific Railway crosses the Little Missouri River was gathered, or scattered, a community — if such institutions as a saloon and a gambling hell and the nominal authority of a sheriff and justice of the peace two hundred miles away make community the right name — such as America produces no longer. Fundamentally its life was like that which has given the historical sagas of Iceland a human attractiveness unsurpassed in literature. Some of the tawdrier elements of modern civilization were indeed there, and gave to the more feeble of its characters and the more dingy of its episodes a greater squalor than that of barbarism; but a little under the surface, among these sinewy people, lay enough of those sound traditions which are the unseen heritage of the civilized, to make not a few of them before long such quiet, sturdy citizens, with a strong streak of generosity in most of them, as have been the pride and are the hope of the West.

In the true saga which a true poet, Mr. Hagedorn, has written there are many arresting figures. The name of Hell-Roaring Bill Jones compels attention: poor Bill Jones — there is really little to say about him, except that his closing days, when drink had taken the lachrymose turn with him, had a milder pathos about them than his august designation might suggest. The almost incredible Marquis de Mores, who was to fall later by the hand of a treacherous Arab ally in Africa, on the threshold of a stupendous design against the hated British Empire, and who at this time was dissipating the millions of his New York father-in-law upon hardly less stupendous designs for the development of Dakota, — they never got beyond design and debt, — plays a larger part in the story. But if such heroes, and the "two-gun men" (gun means pistol), and the real bad men who were noted and heartless man-slayers, and the would-be "bad men" who aped them, and the occasional need, on first introduction, of knocking a man down before his insolence turned to shooting, added a brightness to the social scene, they were far from being the whole of it. Now and then there appeared in it an adventurer of a quite different type, who in another age would have got sainted; the valiant surgeon ministering in perilous journeys to suffering scat-

tered over hundreds of miles, or that tough young
graduate from Michigan who founded and edited
the *Bad Lands' Cowboy*, in a light-hearted championship of decency and reform which went far.

But of course the main element of life was hard
work, and in greatly changed surroundings the
two chosen friends of earlier journeys whom Roosevelt brought out there were much the same men
that they had been as woodmen in far-off Maine,
and his guides and ranching partners, aforemen-
tioned, were not very different from their fathers
who farmed in orderly British New Brunswick.
The fascinating quality of the life lay in this: that,
remote from the reign of law or (very often) of
sound convention either, nearly all the men had
come out there full of hope, nearly all were perforce familiar with danger, toil, and pain, and
nearly all were young.

There was plenty of sport to be had after many
kinds of game. The buffalo had not yet vanished
from that country when Roosevelt came, and on
a long excursion into yet more secluded wilds he
made the much desired acquaintance of the grizzly.
But his full attention was given to ranching in real
earnest, and sharing, to the full extent to which a
master wisely could, the work, privations, and
dangers of his men. All the while what can only

be called the strange physical strength of his brain
allowed him, after hard outdoor days, to enjoy,
for example, Shelley, undisturbed by almost any
surroundings short of the attentions of a skunk,
or to read — likewise to write — much history.

Order was gradually establishing itself. Naturally at first it was promoted more by a voluntary
organization of Western cattle farmers against the
cattle thieves than by public authority. Roosevelt
did much for that organization. He became also
an officer of the law and astounded all that region
of the world by an example of how seriously a man
might take the law. One "Red-Head" Finnigan, —
who boasted that he came "from Bitter Creek where
the further up you went the worse men got" and
that he lived "at the fountain head," — with two
other men stole his boat. He and his men built
another, pursued him down the river, swollen high
but still ice-obstructed, caught and captured the
thieves, and then, when local practice would have
prescribed an immediate hanging, added hundreds
of miles to a terrible journey, just to lodge them in
the gaol. Matthew Arnold would hardly have
believed it, — though Tolstoi easily might, — but
the works of those two authors were the chief
comforts of that expedition. If one were to add
here instances of the abrupt courage with which

he sometimes stopped formidable men's foul mouths, or went out of his way to shame some mean oppressor of Indians, they might, quite delusively, suggest the good boy of an improving story. I will risk impertinence and cite that kindly and gracious gentleman, Mr. Lincoln Lang, ex-cowpuncher, as a witness to the tactful gravity with which he could steady some younger fellow. The exuberant fun of an overgrown schoolboy ran through it all. And there was then, and ever after, the solemn and harmless vanity of a schoolboy there. It showed itself in his smart cowpuncher costume, and in the photographs which he got taken of himself in character. It did not sink in very deep. He knew, perhaps exaggerated, the fact that he was not such a hunter as some men, could not handle a vicious horse like some others, much less fell trees like his Maine friends. But he had tried himself and proved that in the hardest life he could hold his own all round very well. There was no harm in it if he was hugely pleased. He had learned much and could feel himself a real man. Beyond the healing influence of wild nature upon sorrow, these were the very things which he had come for. But he had accomplished something further for other men and for himself. Undesignedly, by holding his own in their pursuits and being a good fellow among them, he had brought into not a few men's lives contact with a range of knowledge, a breadth of vision, and a rigorous standard of right, of which some had never dreamed and others were forgetting the possibility. Because of that contact with a few and the wider reputation which came from it, he was to find himself later a popular leader of an unique — surely a most precious — kind.

III

NEW YORK, WASHINGTON, AND CUBA

ROOSEVELT'S plain friends on his ranches reminded him that bigger things than cattle-farming awaited him and that he must not linger there too long. Perhaps he needed no reminder. He had never lost touch with things in the East. In the autumn of 1886 he let himself be nominated for the mayoralty of New York, a great administrative post in which recurrent reform movements place remarkable men, who accomplish some lasting good and in a little while fall, defeated through the disappointment of impracticable reformers — combined with the hatred of those whom reform hurts. But Roosevelt had offended, as has been seen, the kind of men who accomplished these reforming triumphs, and (besides that once famous theorist Henry George) there was a highly reputable Democratic candidate, who was almost bound to get in. This foreseen failure, however, was quickly followed by great changes in his life.

On December 2, 1886, he married Edith Kermit Carow of New York. Oddly enough he was fulfilling an intention which he had once declared when he was a very little boy. Curiously, too, he was married in London, at St. George's, Hanover Square, feeling, as he said, like a character in Thackeray; and his "best man" was Cecil Spring-Rice, whom, it is to be hoped, Washington remembers and England has not forgotten. Of the happiness that then began no more need be said.

In the next two years some of the best of his books began to appear, and though he more than once visited the ranches, his life, doubtless for his good, was for a while quiet enough. Then, in May 1889, his twenty years of service in responsible public offices began. President Harrison appointed him a member of the United States Civil Service Commission, in which post President Cleveland continued him. In May 1895, he resigned it upon his appointment as Police Commissioner of New York City by Mayor Strong, one of the reforming mayors already alluded to. In April 1897, at the instance of Senator Lodge, the very estimable new President McKinley, not without fear of Roosevelt's supposed impulsiveness, made him Assistant-Secretary of the Navy. The Spanish War began in April 1898. With a compelling inspiration that he must serve in it, Roosevelt resigned from his Navy post, raised a regiment of Rough Riders in the West, as his many friendships there enabled him to do, and served with them, at first under General

Leonard Wood, and soon, upon that officer's promotion, as himself their Colonel.

The distinction which he gained was spectacular enough, and the confidence of most reasonable reformers in him was sufficiently restored, to make him the only possible candidate of the Republican party-machine in New York State, then alarmed about its prospects, for the great office of Governor there. This office he filled for two years. He wished to be reëlected to it. But the Republican potentate of New York State wished him elsewhere, and a wide-spread public opinion in the West desired to have his name on the "Presidential ticket" which it was to vote in 1900. Thus, against his expressed will and the wishes of McKinley, he was nominated for the Vice-Presidency, while McKinley was again nominated for the Presidency. He served the cause of McKinley well by a famous tour of campaigning speeches. The two were elected, and he was considering a further study of law, and perhaps finding some comfort in the dignity of a peculiarly impotent office forced upon him because it was impotent, when on September 6, 1901, an anarchist shot one of the best loved of Presidents, and his tranquil passing away on September 14 left Roosevelt President in his stead.

In Roosevelt's successive public offices, up to

1900, he handled affairs of which any adequate study would take us deep into the political and social history of America. He took his line, too, on some great issues to which one must later return. But his good services are obvious, and so is the ripe administrative experience which he gained. Points for controversy arise but they are essentially the same as will arise later on. Thus the brevity of the notes which follow will not hide the distinction of the career with which they deal.

The system under which every employment in the public service was a favor given through the influence of the powerful to their friends, irrespective of merit, grew to goodly proportions in England when Parliament began to oust the power of the King. It is, however, so totally extinct that we hardly recall how long it lingered. It is probably one hundred and sixty years since the gross cruelty of depriving poor working-folk of their living upon a change of Ministry would have been tolerated here; as a system it never had been tolerated; nor has the dismissal of good officials, once appointed, ever since then been a trouble here. But in the higher walks of public work, though modern needs had long created a prejudice in favor of efficiency, it required the battering-power of Mr. Gladstone, at the zenith of his strength, to make

way for a thoroughly sound method of appointment in the Civil and Military Services — and, by
the way, the names of Roosevelt's friend, Sir
George Trevelyan, and of his father, Sir Charles,
must be associated with Mr. Gladstone's in this.
One almost pathetic little survival of the old order
remained till 1894 and the present writer has had,
as the local M.P. of the party in power, to settle
that the people of a village should post their letters
at the shop of a sound Radical rather than at the
rather more conveniently placed shop of an equally
estimable Unionist. It was the merest survival of
a system practically long extinct.

In America the "spoils system" came into vigor
when democracy came fully to its own. The original
"turning the rascals out" was perhaps sincerely
regarded as a victory over the corruption of the
past, but a foul evil immediately struck its roots
far and wide and deep; and, since neither the direct
injuries to the public nor the sufferings of dis-
possessed officials were at first so prevalent or so
serious as they would have been here, and are in
modern cities of America now, generations grew
up who accepted it (as equally evil things have been
accepted elsewhere) almost as one of the natural
beauties of America. Moreover, the genial but
slack-minded belief that one's self or almost any

one is fit for almost any task is associated with a better instinct; and American contentment with inefficiency, in many things which countries with far less advantages do better, finds plausible excuse in the many cases of exceptional men, who do magnificent work for which their past might seem not to have prepared them. Thus when Roosevelt, as a Civil Service Commissioner, was called to take part in the gradual and partial warring down of this old abuse, the victory of sound principle was far from assured, though the gallantly sustained fight had achieved a good deal through the help of Presidents Hayes, Arthur, and Cleveland. There was now a Civil Service Commission which could and did apply to the candidates for many appointments the rough but useful test of suitable examinations. But the extent to which its services were used in making appointments depended on rules made by the executive and the good-will with which administrators carried them out. Congress could at any time cut down the money appropriated for examinations. Sheerly base opposition to reform was vigorous. A President of either party could not act squarely up to his principles without genuine resentment from the mass of his regular supporters; and even able men of strong and estimable character believed that the public service could be better run without the meddlesome reforms of "long-haired cranks."

The cause of the "long-haired cranks" was in this case one to rouse Roosevelt's enthusiasm in its favor. His studies had taught him what efficient government means. His venture in politics had taught him that worse evils than administrative feebleness arose from the spoils system, through the huge advantage given to corrupt manipulators of politics against any real expression of the people's opinion, and through the wide diffusion of a depraved and cynical tone. Then, too, he was a man sensitive to the manner in which the iron of evil government actually enters into the souls of individual sufferers. Cases like that of a widow struggling for years at some salaried post in a Washington department, faithfully earning enough to maintain her children, and then chucked out despite the protests of her superiors to put a little job into a certain senator's gift, were just the sort of thing to enrage him. And the assistance which the cause then needed was that of a fearless hard-hitter in that office. Supported by his colleagues, he came down unsparingly upon lax and treacherous application of the Civil-Service rules in local customs- or post-offices; prosecuted offenders who had never dreamed that the law would be

enforced against them; paid no deference at all
to a Cabinet Minister, the then famous Postmaster-
General; delighted in confuting before committees
the lies which congressmen concocted about the
examination system; and, when some great Senator, who had attacked the Commissioners and had
been challenged to substantiate his charge, judi-
ciously chose a moment at which Roosevelt was to
have been absent for doing so, suddenly returned a
thousand miles or so to discomfit him. The system had to be proved a reality by very vigorous
enforcement, and the public mind had to be educated to the idea underlying it. For the latter
purpose it was as well that Roosevelt, who could
act very noiselessly at times, had a great facility,
when he chose, for doing things in a way that
made a stir.

The work of President of the Police Commission
of New York, which after six years tempted Roosevelt away from the Civil Service Department, had
a more appealing human interest. The Street-
Cleaning Department of the city, though probably
giving ample scope for a reformer, had not appealed
to him; whereas Mr. Jacob Riis's book, *How the
Other Half Lives*, had long before turned his mind
to things dreadfully wrong in poor city homes,
which good police and sanitation could in some

degree help. His new office gave him a seat also on the Health Board. Whatever may be the case now in a city which the years since have greatly beautified, — incidentally paving it, — New York in the past had no great name for municipal purity. The clumsiness of its institutions went far to ensure evil. The Police Department in particular "represented," as Roosevelt says, "that device of old-school American political thought, the desire to establish checks and balances so elaborate that no man shall have power enough to do anything very bad. In practice this always means that no man has power enough to do anything good, and that what is bad is done anyhow." The constitution of his own Board, and the limitations on its power even when it was united, exposed Roosevelt to being thwarted at every turn by intrigue, though the trouble which he could make when thwarted led to a reform of the system soon after. His problem, which sounds simple, that the police should enforce the law, was in fact one of extreme complexity. Under any system, the police of so strange an aggregate of people as constitutes New York must have a task of stupendous difficulty, much danger, temptation intense and unremitting. With great forces of corruption ever in wait for them, and a feeble system of command above them, their

standard of duty was dragged down by the abundance of laws and ordinances which were merely
vexatious, could not be thoroughly enforced, and
might so reasonably be left idle to oblige some one
— more particularly some one who obliged in
return. In any case bribery and blackmail flour-
ished. "A very large revenue," writes Mr. Bishop,
"was collected by the force from vice and crime
and the unlawful sale of liquor, and this was divided among the higher officials of the force and
the political leaders."

Not to multiply instances — Roosevelt's decisive
(or partly decisive) battle was fought to enforce
the Sunday-Closing Law. Nearly every saloon was
kept open in violation of the law, a price of course
being duly paid for the privilege. It was held impossible to enforce the law. Of course it was
possible for a resolute head of police who gave his
mind to it — provided, that is, that he struck before intrigue to thwart him could collect its
strength, and provided, further, that he had steeled
himself to face the sustained malignity with which
every interest in evil would thenceforth pursue him.
So Roosevelt announced that he should enforce the
law, and he did it. He continued, with a notable
effect upon crime, till his success was partly re-
versed by magistrates who held that one sandwich

plus innumerable drinks was equal not to a drink but to a meal. If the liquor law was thus again evaded, a heavy blow had still been struck at the system of blackmail, and the dormant morale of the force had been aroused.

All along the line Roosevelt was able during his two years in this office to give to the law something of that meaning which it possesses alike in London and in a thousand of the smaller American towns. Statistics and the testimony of severe and knowing critics show this. We need notice here only that this success was due to something more than energetic and astute administration. He was keenly aware that the demoralized force put under him consisted in very large part of splendid human material; including indeed men who were only physically fit, but including far more who were dishonest not from preference but from the continual pressure of none but a dishonest standard set before them; including many, too, who were anything but dishonest, and an astonishingly numerous few who would, upon any call, do deeds of heroism. One cannot, I think, read Roosevelt's own account of his men without seeing something of the heart of the man and, perhaps, revising one's sense of the real problem of goodness in this world.

It is difficult not to regret that Roosevelt passed
so soon from work so closely related to those
philanthropic and religious labors which, though
obviously not his own appointed task, received
much of his inspiring sympathy, back into the narrower world of a Government department in a
capital. But the Navy Department was not a
narrow world to him, and its work, unlike that of
municipal and social reform, was one for which,
if he could have held it for long in a period of
peaceful preparation, his qualifications would have
been unique. Very few Americans can have learned
what his keen reading of history had taught him
— why a great nation generally wants a fleet, and
what manner and size of fleet it wants; though
oddly enough it is to an American—Mahan, author
also of one of the few great biographies of great
Englishmen—that Englishmen, with their proud
naval tradition, themselves owe any clear ideas in
this matter. His actual services to naval efficiency
need not detain us; he was little more than a year
in that office; he had already done much to encourage interest in the sea power, in the course of that
ceaseless writing which must be understood as generally going along side by side with what is here
recorded; but it was later, as President, that in the
matter of marksmanship and in other ways, he

was able to do most for the Navy. But the war with
Spain was looming up, and he did one brilliant
stroke when he contrived that the command of the
Pacific squadron should go to Dewey, a commander
whose action at Manila was like certain feats of
Blake and Nelson, and quite unlike what an average,
prudent, senior officer would have done. All the
while Roosevelt wanted that war to begin; but his
views as a statesman in regard to the Spanish War
and kindred matters form a subject which will
engage us further on — a great and a controversial
subject.

The part which he played in the war need not be
matter of controversy. He had English and American friends who regretted that he left a post where
he had great work to do, to go soldiering, to which
he had no call. This is really to overlook his own
conviction of his own calling. Most of his utterances display his simple conviction that he had
something to teach, a mark which he believed he
might make upon the ideas of growing America,
indeed of young men anywhere. He had said
loudly and often that men should be prepared to
fight and die for their country. He was not forty;
he was extraordinarily strong; it was in peace time
chiefly, we may add, that his driving-power was
badly needed in his department, whereas there was

in fact a particular service which he could render in Cuba. He reflected, as he tells us, that after what he had preached he could not rightly stay at home. When we consider his real situation, it is evident that no man with a soundly sensitive conscience could have felt otherwise. Nor is there any sense in suggesting that he went into it for the fun, which, being in it, he doubtless got out of it, or for the useful popularity which it would bring him. Mature men, who have had real occasion to know that shots do sometimes kill one, do not act on those motives. Roosevelt loved life, and supremely loved his home, nor can anyone doubt his avowal that the thought of the great separation which might happen was awful to him then. And whatever his ambition was, and whatever a man may mean by glory, the idea (which has actually been conceived) of his going into battle in hopes of electioneering réclame, is senseless.

When the "First United States Volunteer Cavalry," one of three such regiments authorized by Congress, was raised, it was a relief to Roosevelt that the nickname "Rough Riders" got attached to it; he had trembled to think that it might be "Teddy's Terrors." The average of them would probably have been rather gratified by this last title, but there is no doubt at all of their devotion

to Roosevelt. He and they played a creditable part
in the fighting which caused the surrender of San-
tiago, and was thus decisive of this short war.
Whether reports which belittled their services
sprang from political jealousy or from the jealousy
which sometimes invades even military breasts,
they are in either case untrue. Roosevelt's happiness about their achievements was expansive and
resounding enough to justify a smile, provided it is
a kindly smile. But anyone, who has ever had
even the slightest acquaintance with bush fighting
and has heard different men tell of their doings in
it, will recognize his account of his fighting experiences as a transparently truthful and modest story.

With his martial glories enhanced by duly insub-
ordinate but effective intervention to get his own
troops and others brought home again before they
died of fever, he returned to become Governor of
New York State. English readers know or should
know that a State is independent and supreme in
most domestic affairs (though the exact line between
its authority and that of the National Government
has become unintelligible now), and that the
functions of a Governor in his State are closely
similar to those of the President in the Union.
The great achievement of Roosevelt's Governorship
was suggested by his experiences in the Legislature

long before. He procured the passing of an Act to require the taxation, as real estate, of all rights over land granted by the Legislature to any Corporation (or, as we say, Company). He procured it by the most strenuous use of that driving-power over the Legislature which a Governor can exercise if he can arouse public opinion to support him, and against the fiercest opposition from powerful interests and his own party-machine. It was a heavy blow dealt to the standing alliance between business interests and party wire-pullers.

Let it be added that the principal other achievements of his contentious Governorship were concerned with the appointment of capable public officers instead of corrupt partisan officers, and that he won his fights over them. It is amazing that, nevertheless, from the commencement of his candidature to the expiry of his office, a noteworthy band of reforming zealots opposed and denounced him, on the ground that he was subservient to the party-machine. The main facts are simple and instructive. Mr. Platt, a strange character, not fond of money, fond of arid theology, and passionately devoted to power, ruled the Republican machine and conceived himself as the *de jure* ruler of the State. When hard fortune drove him to run Roosevelt as a candidate, he tried to make his bargain. Would Roosevelt duly consult him about all appointments and all policies? The answer, given politely but with quite astonishing directness, was that Roosevelt would always consult him, and always, after consulting him, do exactly what he, Roosevelt, thought right. The promise to consult him was fulfilled. The promise to act independently of his advice, and for public interests not those of party, was fulfilled also — there is no question about this — to the letter, though Mr. Platt was pretty constantly using the fiercest threats of political ruin to him. What especially enraged the reforming zealots was this: Platt was an old man and ailing, Roosevelt was young and very well; so, for the purposes of the promised consultations, the Governor went to the Boss's house in New York instead of dragging the old man to Albany to visit him. This merely shows that Governor Roosevelt was a gentleman.

Looking forward to his later conduct we should take note of two lasting but conflicting impressions now made upon him, or rather reinforced; one was of deep public resentment against the rich corporations and their political influence; the other of more superficial but still acute irritation against a certain breed of theoretical reformers, who dream that one can influence the world for good while dwelling afar from that inelegant place. And we should no less note that from the beginning to the end of this very pure early career, every good thing that it had been given to Roosevelt to do had — so it happened — been a matter of sheer hard fighting.

Roosevelt had thus, before he was forty-three, already lived one of the lives that are worth recording. At that point a tragic event placed him in one of the most eminent positions in the world, at a time when a powerful man set there had to do with things of no common importance. Thenceforward he was to live — not that he had any reluctance so to live — under "that fierce light which beats upon a throne" and continues to follow, though with diminishing brightness, kings and such when they have lost their place. His vehement deeds while in place and his no less vehement protests amid events of graver moment afterward present a series of controverted matters, worth controversy and to be fairly faced. It may be well to pause here and note some things which help to show by what standards, thenceforth, he should be judged — what could fairly be demanded of him and what not.

He was not a man of genius, however we may define that mysterious quality which, among statesmen of recent times, we see clearly in Lincoln, and which at least those who remember his living presence must ascribe to Gladstone. Self-centred as he was, in the sense that among other natural phenomena his own individual self rather fascinated and on the whole pleased him, he had a paradoxical but very true kind of modesty, and repeatedly called attention to the fact that he was not a man of genius. This was worth calling attention to, because plenty of people around him rated him extravagantly. It is still worth calling attention to, because nature and accident combined to make him a spectacular figure, and critics have become pettily carping about him on not finding what they never need have looked for.

He had none the less such varied and extraordinary powers (powers some or all of which may be lacking in a man of genius) as may perhaps never have been possessed in combination by any other man. He certainly did not let them lie idle; he used them unsparingly — prodigally. We must think later whether on the whole he used them for high aims and with God's blessing. Among his gifts, his great bodily efficiency, along with the forcible bearing which it facilitated, bulks so largely in some people's eyes that they think there was little more of him and imagine that he valued it overmuch. In reality, though his conservation

of bodily vigor and prowess to the verge of old age
was rare and admirable, his just estimate, for himself and for his sons (in his letters to them), of the
true and subordinate value of that side of life was
rarer and more admirable. And while many remarkable men have been his athletic equals, very few,
whether physically vigorous or only mentally so,
have equaled him in certain mental endowments,
or in the exuberant delight with which he used
them. In particular the rapidity with which he
read, his memory for what he had once thus
rapidly read, and the ease with which after bodily
fatigue or in the midst of earnest cares he could
turn to any kind of study, were all but unexampled.
Macaulay, whom he loved, had some of these facul-
ties; Gladstone, whom, for all the contrasts between
them, he obviously admired, was perhaps his only
equal among famous men in undefeated, all-round
vitality. Equipped with these powers, he galloped
over vast tracts of historical and biological knowledge, of poetry and of romance, delighting in them
as he delighted in his sports — delighting in them
far more, if one may judge from the men of whom
he sought and won intimacy.

It was an exuberant delight, showing that peren-
nial boyishness on which the best of his biographers
have insisted. He was eager to meet the most

learned men in subjects of which his learning
amounted to something; when he met them it was
with less desire to listen to them than to exercise
his own knowledge, sound and unsound. How
many of us must have caught ourselves doing the
like! So, occasionally, he gave himself away. His
books vary very much in quality — and he wrote
a good deal for his living. He confessedly scamped
the last part of his "Benton," which does not
matter, and when he wrote of the history of the
West, telling with great vivacity and justice about
matters of ever fresh interest, the very learned say
that he had not dug in Spanish archives. He could
be plausibly accused of platitude; his emphatic
way invited it, and so did his simple words. English statesmen of the very first rank may occur
to us who have in our time written serious books
or given scholarly discourses. It would be rash to
maintain that any one of them (with a doubtful
exception for some who have been men of letters
first) has written stuff of more real value than
Roosevelt, or so seldom been entirely shallow.
Certainly in this island, where statesmanship has
long been associated with scholarly attainments,
no statesman for centuries has had his width of
intellectual range. And his was vitalized knowledge, illuminating practical life at numberless

points.   But this is not to say that he had a deeply
reflective mind.   We are told that in great practical affairs he would willingly take counsel, but
ultimately made up his mind by a flashing sort of
intuitive process; sometimes prefaced by repeated
self-contradiction; very often obviously right; but
in almost all cases without a logic perceptible to
other men.   Thus neither a gospel nor a philosophy
can be made out of his words or example, though
they might illustrate at many points an old, old
gospel or philosophy.   With just views on matters
that happened to engage his interest, he could dis-
pose of some, such as the tariff question, which did
not, in phrases packed with meaninglessness such
as he later attributed to Mr. Wilson.   It matters
little, if, after all, he more often than most of us
did the right thing bravely.

Physically and mentally he showed a phenome-
nally quick response of act to stimulus, such as a
great boxer exhibits.   Let us add to this that he
spent his life — largely, by no means solely — in
fighting, and that quite obviously up to his Presidency it was fighting against evil things.   In the
far more complex and exacting struggles of his
after years, it is not to be supposed that he would
never pick the wrong man to assail, never assail
him with the first weapon that came handy, never

carry the assault ruthlessly far. It should be enough
to find, if we do find it, that a broad generosity
pervaded his life; that he still by preference smote
the cruel and the foul; that that instant response
to stimulus, which would leave him in some ways
no more unsoiled than most statesmen, could result
also in instant self-sacrifice when most would
have faltered.

Finally, of course he was ambitious. But so far
it had been a strange course of ambition. Of the
seven civil offices which he held, every one had
come to him through the unsolicited choice of him
by some one else. And in all his career so far,
the several bold departures made upon his own
initiative, though they turned to his advantage,
were all rash acts from which friends would have
dissuaded him and which could hardly have suggested themselves to any commonly scheming man's
mind. The freely censured courses of his later years
should be judged in the light of this. It should be
candidly recognized forthwith that he possessed
an ambition of a rare sort — the ambition, not
particularly for the President's place or any other,
or for wealth, or even fame, or even power, but to
live to the full the life of a man.

How good is man's life, the mere living!

He wrote these words of Browning's early in one

of his hunting books. Presumably he did not
always live — for the best of us do not — quite on
the same high level. But, at the end of the story
we may think — though I shall not labor the
point with argument — whether upon the whole,
as the temptations of high station and middle age
multiplied, there was falling off of aspiration,
or whether, rather, this love of living mellowed
into the love of a larger life than that youthful
quotation or this political biography tells of.

IV

NINETEENTH–CENTURY AMERICA

The few years just before Roosevelt became President may fairly be looked upon as closing one period and beginning another in the history of the United States. It may be best to hazard here some crude and hasty remarks upon the course of the nation's development up till then. They will not be concerned with the romantic or tragic element in American history, that long-drawn struggle for making good the Union and for extirpating slavery, which affords a marked sequence of events and in which the work of strong personalities for good or evil is peculiarly easy to trace. This had reached its memorable climax while Roosevelt was a little boy.

Side by side with it, or rather blending with it and determining the course of the struggle, there had proceeded a movement displaying itself at first in the adventures of rugged and frugal pioneers, and culminating in the colossal performances of financier princes, sometimes invincibly unscrupulous, sometimes gigantically munificent, or, sometimes, both. In its earlier stages it is called the Winning of the West; its concluding stage was the fashioning of a huge, amorphous dominion into an economic organism, richer far than any before it. Its pioneers belong to the past; so may, possibly before long, its princes. A great multitude of plain people, reasonably prosperous but not enchained by material prosperity, established over a wide region which the barrier of the Allegheny Mountains may be said to veil from many eyes in Europe and, perhaps, even some in the Eastern States, is its most enduring and truly distinguished result.

The immense size of the United States has always had an influence on its character, in many ways which a little imagination will suggest; perhaps the drawback which it was bound to impose upon some kinds of progress and on the growth of an alert and well-informed public opinion (such as England, which in some ways might appear a less educated country, may be credited with) is not sufficiently allowed for by Americans who are impatient with their own land. One great effect of that size, together with the remarkable natural wealth of the inland stretches remote from the Atlantic, is apparent from what has just been said. America was, well within living memory, a new country in a peculiar sense. As a political entity it is of course older than many other sovereign states, far older than the French Republic, the late German Empire, or the Kingdom of Italy. In social respects a State like New Zealand, though settled only in our fathers' days, may by now have set up anew every essential element in the life of the country from which it was derived. Indeed, individually considered, Boston, Baltimore, Charleston, and a hundred other cities or communities in the United States are older than so great an English city as Birmingham; they look older, and are at least as redolent of a matured and mellow civilization. But in the life of the whole nation, powerful as is and always must be the influence of that old America and of traditions as deeply rooted in it as in England itself, an influence not less strong was exercised, from the time of the Revolution onward, by the growing population of a newly settled area along a frontier ever advancing toward the west.

The quick rise of a thoroughly democratic government in America was due less to principles taught in France, or to the germination in new soil of ideas long dormant in England, than to the facts of actual life in this new community. John Adams's dream of implanting an aristocratic element in the Republic was futile, and even Hamilton's passion for strong government could take little hold on

the public mind, when a growing and vigorous
section of the people lived under conditions which
made equality not a theory but a fact, bred in them
an intense self-reliance, and, at first, gave them no
prospect of getting much help from state authority
even if they had desired it. Such conditions retained
their influence in every part of the inland country
long after its originally wild character had given
place to civilization. They were the foundation
of a democratic system which in the main justified
the pride with which it was spoken of. Doubtless
these same conditions also helped the growth of
practices and methods ill adapted to keep democracy clean and vigorous later. People for whom
government has few things of importance to do
may easily grow content that it should be "a poor
thing but their own." Far more important than
the mistakes and vicious practices which the
fathers of the West helped to fasten upon their
country, and which loom so large in the merely
political history of America, was the ordinary
life of the great sound social democracy which
they created.

The stage of actual pioneer life, of course, passed
quickly enough in each successively settled district; nor is it to be imagined that later settlement,
in the days of great railways and when the more

rugged and thickly wooded regions of the nearer
West had been won, bore much resemblance to
that of earlier days; or even that the development
by capitalistic enterprise of cattle-farming in a still
further West produced quite similar conditions.
The better, or even the average, pioneer farmer
required great qualities, but the West attracted
some who were almost as shiftless as they were
rough; and, as many English families know, a
goodly selection of the scapegraces least wanted
in their own homes have always adorned any kind
of frontier life for a while. Conflict with savage
enemies developed a strain of cruelty and treachery
unsparingly dealt with in Roosevelt's historical
pages, and the strain may not be quite worn out;
yet, as in the somewhat comparable case of English
sea-adventure, the nobler characteristics evoked
have left a deeper mark in the nation's history.
A pioneer population, as distinguished from staider
settlers who follow in its wake, tends in part to
extinguish itself, in part to form in a little while the
best element in a more ordered society.

Nothing could be less suggestive of the wilderness or of savagery now than the wide agricultural regions once called the West, though considerable hardship and isolation remain. Yet what
has been said of the equality, the sense of freedom,

and the indifference to Government, of those Wes-
terners who shocked and prevailed over the more
conservative founders of the Republic, long remained hardly less true of their descendants or suc-
cessors in the Middle West. Few settle as farmers
in a newly opened country except self-reliant and
adaptable men of considerable though orderly
energy. The policy of Government from the first,
wisely no doubt, was to encourage the growth of
population by almost gratuitous grants of land
in equal amounts. The ordinary Western farm is
one hundred and sixty acres, or a quarter of one of
the square-mile sections, bordered by mud roads,
into which a great part of the United States is
mapped. In the central regions of the Mississippi
basin, the fertility of the land is so extraordinary
that it could be cropped with the same crop for a
generation, before manure became necessary or even
useful; with the consequence that a good start
could be made with the little capital which could
easily be borrowed. Thus those ideals of a highly
individualist society, which fascinated European
economists and political philosophers in the middle of the nineteenth century, were fulfilled in
an extraordinary degree in the process by which
the still predominant section of the present American Commonwealth has been built up.

The social problems, which the industrial development and the preceding agricultural development of England brought quickly in their train, had for long no existence for the bulk of America. Of the few things which Western settlers demanded and got from public authority one, however, demands mention. An effective system of elementary education was quickly set up everywhere; and if in some respects the vision of its promoters may seem limited, yet amid these wholesome conditions the simple accomplishment of reading meant, to characters of which Lincoln's is the preëminent example, the power of teaching themselves what no teacher can impart. In one last and supreme respect the temper of the pioneer continues to this day to affect all America. Most families had come from far and adapted themselves to new conditions and tried their hands on new tasks, or remembered how their predecessors and saw how their neighbors had done so. The spirit of such enterprise was an heirloom in the most contented and well-established homes.

This process of land settlement was long drawn out in America, and long continued to have a far greater importance than mercantile or mining developments or the manufacturing ventures which, till a recent time, lived in some real fear of dumping

from England. But in its later stages it drew after
it the growth of a strangely contrasting phenome-
non, capitalist enterprise — meaning, of course,
such enterprise as cannot start at all without
much accumulated money behind it — of unexampled magnitude and audacity. In the first place,
of course, agricultural growth involved that enormous amount of railway construction which had
proceeded far enough by 1870, or soon after, to
make America the chief source of food supplies to
our country, and Europe the great market of Western
farmers till the growth of American manufactures
should provide them with a great market nearer
home. The early era of great railway construction
in England produced some now forgotten scandals.
The era when competing enterprise in America
was rushing along, with less supervision of its
financial operations than exists in the case of our
railways here, covering the West with a network
of parallel or interlacing tracks, is a subject on
which an Englishman, who happens to have received his portion of his father's goods in American railway investments, should not be encouraged
to speak at large. It must, however, be said that
railway rates excited as keen an interest there as
here, were not there at first thought a proper subject for government regulation, have tended to be

low, but have caused bitterness owing to favors given to one trader over another; that the exceedingly difficult question of the relative public advantages of competition and combination had become a burning one by the end of the last century, while public policy was still more hostile to combination than with us; above all, that operations concerned with railways became in the years after the Civil War the source of many large and some gigantic private fortunes. The country had reached by then a stage at which the development of its resources could proceed with great rapidity, if the ambition of able private undertakers applied itself to the task. The construction and management of railways, and therewith the management or manipulation of their finances, offered not of course the only but for some years the most conspicuous field for great adventurers, attracting to it no small share of the outstanding ability of the country.

Of the railwaymen of mark many no doubt were people of high constructive talent, employed with great benefit to the public; some were visionary optimists such as become dishonest when in difficulties; not a few were notable thieves in a country which had not developed its thief-catching machinery to any high degree of efficiency. Anyway the great convulsion and the heroic efforts of the

Civil War were followed by a period in which America corporately was fast becoming the richest nation of the earth, and its average inhabitants were becoming more prosperous than those of any other land; but its leading inhabitants in its own eyes and those of the world were men of abnormal wealth. That wealth compelled attention by its sudden growth, its disproportion to the ordinary rewards of good service, and the difficulty of its scarcely fortunate possessors in enjoying it. It excited disgust through the knowledge that it was often ill-gotten. For a while it might cause in a great number of Americans a keener sense than ever that the world is a place to get rich in, and a duller sense than ever that not all methods that succeed are admirable. But a widespread and deep reaction in men's minds must follow, and by the close of the nineteenth century it was ready to show itself in many ways.

Meanwhile, however, the growth of means of communication had made possible a more startling development of capitalism. It is commonly associated with the name "trusts," but its essence is the replacement of moderate-sized industrial concerns by very large concerns, each with a tendency to swallow up or amalgamate with its business rivals, sometimes a tendency also to acquire and direct the businesses which supply its raw material and the businesses which distribute its products.] Such concerns, of course, demand the services of many gifted subordinates, but they are generally the creation of one man of great and imaginative daring. The building-up of a big business in a special line is of course one thing; the absorption of rivals and the bidding for monopoly is another; but they tend to be combined. There is absorbing interest in the economic study of the conditions which in different countries and at different times are favorable to a big business or set the limit to its growth. Where do the economies derivable from great size end, and where do the unwieldiness and slackness of the overgrown organism begin?

The line must be drawn differently under different conditions, but in more than one respect the conditions of America specially favored gigantic growth. One of these was the facility for marketing (the first essential to big business) afforded by the existence of great multitudes of customers, all easily accessible by railway, all accustomed to ordering goods from far, and with requirements and tastes which in many ways were remarkably uniform. Thus the close similarity of all the farms along hundreds of miles of railway made possible a great "combine" in the agricultural-implements trade.

Beginning soon after 1880, great businesses and great combinations aiming at monopoly came more and more to astonish and alarm America. The advantage or disadvantage of these great organizations to the public who buy from them is a more difficult question than it might be thought. No big business could establish itself except by offering sound goods cheap at the outset. Even if it obtained a monopoly, there would be a point beyond which the raising of prices would mean a loss through the shrinking of custom; and actual monopoly can rarely be reached and still more rarely kept secure. Thus it is questioned whether the purchasing public has ever quite lost the advantage which a very great industrial concern has begun by offering it. So in some degree the enmity which instinct and the tradition of the Common Law aroused against the monopolist or would-be monopolist may have been mistaken.

Essentially it was not far wrong. The experiment, whether a real private monopoly in some necessary commodity would be a great calamity, is one which no sane people would have wished to try out, especially as behind the big industrialists in different lines there began to loom the figures of the great financiers who might imaginably come to control them all. The world is not likely to come entirely into the ownership of a handful of magnates, but it sometimes comes near enough. And the ambition of the man who chooses to be immensely rich must often if not always be of a more or less maniacal kind. Then too, in this process of wealth-getting, it is not only the great industrialist who has given obvious value for what wealth he gets — like Carnegie, the sincere author of the saying that "a man who dies very rich dies disgraced" — who waxes fat. The financier who engineered a combination of a hundred companies might realize possibly more than the total original worth of those companies, by putting upon the market, in the form of shares in a new company, the estimated additional value created by the fact of their combination. Further, apart from the doubtful loss or gain which might result to the consumer from monopoly, there was the unquestionable social loss arising from the quick extinction of a number of smaller ventures. And the process of their extinction was often brutal and base. Sale at a great temporary loss next door to the little business which was to be ruined; every form of malign ingenuity to hamper a rival; corruption of his employees; even, in certain recorded instances, the actual subornation of crime, were the agencies freely used. So it came to pass that in an America once prone to worship the rich, connection even with the administration of Mr. Rockefeller's stupendous and most wisely directed charities became in the popular mind a disqualification for any kind of elective office.

The growth of industry went along with the admission, during many years, of vast swarms of immigrants, drawn no longer as the earlier (largely agricultural) immigration had been from the Northern countries of Europe, but mainly from Southern and Eastern Europe, aggregated in large masses in mining districts and large towns, and apt to preserve for long their own language and national ways. Hence comes the problem of assimilating an alien population, which evokes and justifies passionate insistence (such as that of Roosevelt) upon "Americanism." Hence too labor questions, such as European countries had known earlier, arose in somewhat acute forms and began to agitate relatively excitable and politically uneducated newcomers. Native opinion and that of the earlier comers from England, Ireland, and Germany was not very sympathetic to what we call the cause of Labor.

The real bulk of the country remained on the whole agricultural; talented and enterprising youth from it was drawn increasingly into towns but readily found employment in trade and in the positions of foremen and the like, and was seldom attracted to the exercise of high manual skill. The tending of machinery found handy and generally docile human instruments in the newcomers. Their wages were good, judged by their own old standards extremely good. But rank abuses grew up in many places in a country where both the Federal constitution and the slow awakening of the general public to coming needs kept factory and sanitary law very backward. Great American employers seldom fall into the mistake of supposing that low wages are in themselves an economy; nor American workmen into that of favoring restriction of output. But the cleavage of sympathies between employers and manufacturing or mining wage-earners was somewhat marked and harsh. Strikes were apt to take a violent even a murderous form, such as they had only had in England in a small area and for a short time just before 1870; and strike-breaking could be pretty violent too. The earlier Labor Unions roused antagonism by great mistakes; and, while there was much to make the possible insurrection of labor peculiarly menacing, public opinion had not and has not yet met the idea of labor combination in so tolerant and friendly a spirit as here. Incidentally it may be remarked that the efforts of any Trade Union to force all workers in its trade into its ranks, though acquiesced in here, have excited much displeasure among Americans, including Roosevelt.

The South remained in a temper not yet wholly reconciled and did not yet take its full part in the nation's life; and the riddle of the Negro remained and remains unsolved. That larger view of the relations of North and South and of white and black, which Lincoln possessed, might not have enabled even him to produce great results quickly; but the power had passed with his death to men who, with the pathetic exception of Andrew Johnson, his drunken and undignified successor in office, were totally destitute of his vision.

It may be largely for this reason that the tone of national politics had become for almost a generation depressed. But a very great war, for all its possible glory and nobility of prevalent motive, seems generally to be followed by a period of moral depression, through which the high aspirations which it may have kindled must struggle hard to survive. The physical and spiritual flower of young manhood in the nation concerned has always been in some measure extirpated, while the pacifist and the profiteer remain and flourish. More important still, the high enthusiasms which such a war stirred

up do not easily find their appointed outlet in the
vaguer and more perplexing problems of returning
peace; so that in many they are quenched. All the
time mediocre natures have been driven by public
anxiety to a keener zest for vulgar pleasures. Anyhow the Civil War was no exception to the common
rule in this: that the period immediately following
it was not felt to be one of general moral uplifting.
Coming as it did moreover upon public departments
little trained to cope with such matters, and coin-
ciding as it did in its later stages with a great
growth of trade, the Civil War contributed something, by scandals connected with war contracts,
to the magnification of dishonesty in business.

In spite of occasional acute depression, the time
that followed was one of brilliant business growth
which must in any case have brought temptations.
The political party to which the triumph of the
Union seemed to give a title to long unshaken
power could long bank upon its past record of
usefulness. It was in the main also the party of the
solid business interests, and the progress of the
country seemed mainly to depend upon assuring the
prosperity of those interests. A certain flatness
of political tone was perhaps inevitable. Without
assuming for a moment that the prominent persons
of the time were in the main at all unworthy per-

sons, an outsider may note the fact that to the outside world the surface aspect of American life, at this time of great progress in wealth, was in some respects slightly gaudy and in others decidedly dingy, and may conjecture that this was far more acutely felt in America, though undoubtedly a change for the better, in matters to which allusion has been made, had become manifest some time before the end of the century. American intellect, outside business affairs, added to the general aspect of depression, prone as it became to a self-conscious and over elaborate culture with no root in the soil of common life, and tempted as were some of its votaries to the not very noble desire to be English rather than American.

Such or in some degree such — for I would repeat how fully conscious I am of the crudeness and probable inaccuracy as well as the fragmentary nature of this survey — had been the period which was beginning to pass when high authority and leadership came to Roosevelt — to a man conversant and sympathetic in a rare degree with the many different sections of his country, alive to its latent greatness and its actual shortcomings, qualified to play a man's part (not a superman's) in the manifold kinds of progress upon which the hearts of thousands besides himself were set.

V

DOMESTIC AFFAIRS DURING ROOSEVELT'S PRESIDENCY

NOTHING could have been further from Roosevelt's intentions than to set up as the prophet of some great Reformation or make a violent breach with the past. Some ardent souls among his friends may have been a little disappointed when, upon taking the oath of office, he announced that he would retain McKinley's Cabinet instead of surrounding himself with men of his own choice, and would continue McKinley's policies — which indeed he had been elected Vice-President to do. He was not alarmed at being called "a pale copy of McKinley." "If," he said afterwards, "a man is fit to be President, he will so impress himself on the office that the policies pursued will be his anyhow." The originality which in fact he displayed in facing the problems that arose for him, lay chiefly in that high and vivacious courage with which he reënforced an honesty not lacking in his predecessors.

Before touching singly on some of the issues with which he dealt, — confining ourselves in the present chapter to domestic issues, — we may consider his general relations with the Republican party, of which the ostensible leadership had devolved upon him. It had come into being nearly fifty years before as the party of progress. It was now the party which had preserved the Union and under which an extraordinary growth of wealth had occurred. The claim to be called the party of progress might for a while seem to have passed to the Democrats. But the strong and upright President Cleveland had ended at outs with his party, and from 1896 onward the Democratic party, taken as a whole, represented to Roosevelt a combination of unthinking conservatism in some respects with reckless demagogism in others. Except for an interval under Jackson's leadership, it had always stickled for the rights of the States against the National Government and the strict limitation of the latter's powers — principles which were great obstacles to dealing with urgent industrial questions. But in 1896 the theory of bimetallism (much in favor then with Lord Chaplin, as the farmers' friend, and with others in England) offered a new disguise for the oldest of quack remedies for popular discontents, debasing the currency. Not to mention the views of the silver-miners, Western farmers, suffering from fallen prices while their mortgage interest remained as before, offered a field for

agitation. Whatever may be the true extent of
the advantage of a system of bimetallism by international agreement, such as McKinley like many
English statesmen advocated, it is certain that the
silver proposals with which Mr. Bryan then bade
fair to stampede the West would have worked wide-
spread disaster. And the spirit of his amazing eloquence, inflamed by such sincerity as the truly
rhetorical temperament is capable of, — "you shall
not crucify mankind upon a cross of gold," and so
forth, — was that of unredeemed claptrap with all
its cruel potency of harm.

In 1900 the Democratic party, as a party, still
meant Mr. Bryan, though its war cry for the
moment had been mere condemnation of McKinley's foreign policy, to which we must turn in the
next chapter. Roosevelt, with his view of that
policy, was bound to regard the Republican party
as in effect the party of honest policy, which had
now for the second time fought and won a battle
for the honest cause as such, against an altogether
spurious radicalism. "This," however, as he wrote
twelve years later, "regrettably, but perhaps inevi-
tably, tended to throw the party into the hands
not merely of the conservatives but of the reaction-
aries: of men who sometimes for personal and
improper reasons, but more often with entire sin-

cerity and uprightness of purpose, distrusted anything that was progressive and dreaded radicalism."
This was a just analysis. And we may regard it as
Roosevelt's chief political ambition, up to a certain moment in 1912, to make the party, which he
deemed on the whole that of essential sanity, the
ready instrument of practical and, at need, of
radical reforms.

This meant at the outset that he should coöperate
as far as possible, though steadily increasing fric-
tion was bound to come, with established leaders
of his party, especially in the Senate and the
House. With his own Cabinet loyal fellow-working
was assured. Few Presidents can have been more
fortunate than he was in the men (more particularly John Hay, Mr. Taft, and Mr. Root) whose
chief he was. And — which seems the mark
of great Presidents — he welcomed strong men in
his Cabinet, maintaining even daily intercourse
with any departmental chief whose business
made it desirable; governed by advice or going
his own way, and leaving his subordinates free
or taking the whole responsibility for great
decisions off them, as the needs of the moment
made fitting; and eagerly claiming for them the
credit for their work. But his fearless nature went
a long way to make him a good worker with

any man with whom it was possible to work.

Anecdotes abound, indeed, of the comical vigor with which he would denounce, in any hearing, weighty personages and even august bodies who conflicted with him; they were accused of not knowing, when the roll of their grave assembly was called, whether to answer "present" or "not guilty"; or they were made life members of the "Ananias Club," sometimes for more serious inaccuracies than that of Ananias, but sometimes, it appears, for relating only too accurately what honorable men would have treated as a confidence. Spiteful critics delighted to point out that Roosevelt all the while would enter into practical relations with the very kind of men that he thus unrestrainedly denounced. But quite enough of his correspondence is now before the world to set his conduct in these regards in a clear light. His refusal to conciliate any one, in appointments or any other matter, at the expense of what — in his own judgment — the public interest required was expressed with an instant and astonishing frankness which left no room for mistake. But, that line being once plainly drawn, he had no Pharisaic reluctance to going along with any man just so far as their ways lay together, even with a man whom he openly condemned, when that man happened to be working for a good end. Thus, when by a malicious trick the management in the Senate of a bill which he promoted was thrown by its opponents into the hands of a Senator whom he had publicly stamped with his disapproval but who supported the bill, Roosevelt felt no trace of the embarrassment by which almost any other man would have been hampered.

This, which it would be easy to illustrate further, is not merely an honorable but a beautiful trait. To speak broadly, it seems beyond question that Roosevelt with unflinching courage departed all along the line from tradition which had, in many ways, bound down Presidents to consulting the greatest number of private interests where the single public interest should have been plain; but, in doing so, he sought to disturb as little as might be the harmony of those relations with his party without which he would have been powerless for good. It would be peddling to enquire whether on some occasion or another he conceded what he need not have conceded. This man from an early time had thrown away any advantage that could ever be his from mean compliance with mean people.

Of his dealings with men there is one outstanding example, in his relations with a person who was anything but mean, the once famous Senator Mark

Hanna. This once much-abused potentate, who had made McKinley President and was reputed to hold his party in the hollow of his hand, was, we may take it, the type of those Republicans whom Roosevelt respected and disagreed with. Nobody will now defend all Hanna's principles of action, as he himself fearlessly did, though many may still act upon them: The party had saved the Union and business prospered under it; the party must win, and must win at all costs. If, as is very freely suggested, Hanna carried out this principle almost as thoroughly as, say, Sir Robert Walpole in the eighteenth century, it must be remembered that there is a real analogy between the points of view of the English Whig Minister with the exiled Stuart dynasty still threatening, and of this Republican stalwart. In one cause at least, that of conciliation between capital and labor, he and Roosevelt could work together whole-heartedly, and when they did not differ openly each knew that the other was loyal to him. But Hanna was plainly shown that his influence was at an end in the very first appointment of a kind which he had previously controlled, and in the policy in regard to trusts which the new President avowed from the outset.

Before long the two were the recognized leaders of two opposing tendencies in the party, and the

question was bound to arise whether the next
Republican candidate for the Presidency should
be Roosevelt, or Hanna himself, or perhaps some
deputy of his. During 1903 a rival of Hanna's
in his own State saw fit to thrust the question forward. Hanna was forced to try to put off a declaration from his own State in Roosevelt's favor.
Instantly and effectively Roosevelt frustrated his
move and secured his own position. A few months
later Hanna lay dying, and the last simple notes between the old chief and Roosevelt remain a significant memorial of the great hearts of two strong men.

Roosevelt was determined, he said, to be "the
President of the whole nation: not of a section," not
of the North (to which his actual words referred)
more than of the South; not of the white men,
to the exclusion of the Negro or the Indian; not
of business and of the rich, rather than of labor and
of the poor — nor the other way on. No doubt any
man in his place might have used the phrase. The
clue to any just estimate of his presidency lies in his
having fully made good this claim.

It is needless now to revive all the controversies
in which he was involved. It would be enough
to tabulate those actions of his which were in
intent or effect most provocative. It would be seen
at once that, roughly speaking, they balance one

another. He recognizes just Southern claims as no one since the Civil War had done, and goes out of the way to attack the chief thing that was disgracing the South, as hardly any man would have done; he gives the Negro race a peculiarly useful encouragement in the very spirit of Lincoln, and suppresses riotous Negro troops with extreme severity; falls violently upon the misdeeds of men of wealth one day, and attacks lawless labor-agitators to their faces as violently the next day. And in every case he has a good plain reason, given in good dignified English, for what he has done.

In this slight sketch I pass over many details to insist the more emphatically on this one point. It may or it may not be possible to criticize Roosevelt severely on one incident or another of his administration; but if once you set before you as a whole the mass of the criticized transactions, this conclusion leaps to light: the statesman who was censured during eight years for all these particular things needs no further proof that he was a man of splendid justice everlastingly in action — of splendid justice, and with the gift of all-embracing sympathy.

This should be borne in mind while we consider the domestic controversy which filled the largest space in his career, the question of trusts, in the loose sense in which the word means great industrial combinations. Possibly it may be asked why Roosevelt, who took an aggressive attitude on this question, avoided that of the tariff, which some people — probably mistaken — would think a matter of deeper economic and political consequence. A thoroughgoing English free-trader, by the way, approaches the American tariff question with serene impartiality; he must suppose that free trade would be good for America, which has probably long outgrown the stage in which the plea for fostering infant industries has any application; but he must equally suppose that the adoption of free trade by the United States would bring a perilous crisis upon English commerce. Roosevelt, who confessedly and very naturally knew little about this economic question, came to see clearly, later on, how unsatisfactory it was that tariffs should be settled by the process — which then prevailed — of barter, between powerful interests, in committees. On becoming President he considered, as we know from Hay, whether he should demand a revision of the tariff. Whatever his own views as to a satisfactory kind of tariff may have been, his deliberate conclusion was that he could not hope to carry his party with him in any handling of the matter that was worth attempting. There can really be

no question that he was right in this. Nor was
there at that moment, or thereafter while he remained President, anything to make immediate
agitation of this question his proper course. We
shall see that it was otherwise with the trusts
question.

The history of this matter can be summed up
briefly. When big trusts began to be heard of, after
the formation of Mr. Rockefeller's oil trust in 1882,
conservative opinion in America was alarmed by
them, and it was easy to pass a law (the Sherman
Act of 1890) by which agreements in restraint of
trade, being at common law void and unenforceable,
were further made the subject of criminal proceedings — in so far, that is, as they concerned commerce between different States and thus came within
the scope of Federal legislation. This disposed of
the original device by which previously competing
companies agreed to deposit their voting-powers in
the hands of a group of trustees (whence the name,
"trusts"). It was sought to evade the law by the
formation of new companies, which acquired and
held a majority of the stock in each of the companies to be combined. In 1894 the proceedings
taken against one of these new combinations failed,
the Supreme Court holding in the "Knight case,"
among other matters, that the buying and holding

of stock in other corporations, which was what the holding companies did, was not "commerce" and thus not within the scope of the Federal power of legislation as to commerce between States. Thereupon, contrary to the intention of the law, a number of large combinations had by 1901 sprung up, each of which was believed by competent lawyers to be justified by the Knight case; and it would appear that the great business-world generally had by this time become interested in such developments.

Roosevelt in his first message to Congress — called by Hay "the most individual message since Lincoln" — declared, without consultation of any man, his general attitude towards the movement. In the changing conditions of trade, combinations of capital were, he said, necessary; they should be regarded in no spirit of envy; but there was a general conviction that in certain of their features and tendencies they were hurtful to the general welfare. Government was bound to see that these powerful agencies worked in harmony with the general welfare. But the first requisite was knowledge and publicity. With a view to this he recommended now the appointment of a new Cabinet officer, the Secretary of Commerce and Labor. This first step, the creation of this officer with a Bureau of Corporations under him, may seem unsensational;

but it was important enough to be opposed by reactionary business-interests with all their power. By vigorous efforts he secured this measure from Congress early in 1903. The new Bureau could investigate; could secure a certain amount of publicity; could recommend necessary measures. That was all, but there seems to be no doubt that it sufficed to check many abuses and to direct much business ambition into useful rather than harmful paths.

Meanwhile, however, Roosevelt was concerned with the associated question of the railways and their rates. A measure forbidding rebates was passed, also in 1903. And in 1906, largely through efforts of his in the course of which he was led to adopt a more advanced view than that with which he started, there was passed an Act giving to the Interstate Commerce Commission — an executive body guided by considerations of policy and only in a small degree restrained by the Courts — drastic and general powers of fixing rates. It is arguable on economic grounds that in the long run rates will fix themselves best of themselves; but in such matters there is always an interest — that of a public of innumerable small people — which can assert itself only through a public agency; nor can popular feeling in the modern world be asked to forgo all public control over capitalist undertakings of vast public import. Roosevelt then was probably right (against that sturdy life-long champion of sound causes, Senator Lodge, his respected friend whether in an agreement or disagreement), in regarding the decision then taken not as leading toward public ownership of the railways but as the best hope of escape from that probably very wasteful form of Socialism. However that may be, the knowledge gained by the Bureau of Corporations and the example set in the case of the Interstate Commerce Commission together pointed the way to the next step in the Big Business problem: namely, to entrust an expert Commission, continuously engaged in the study of all the relevant facts, with large powers of deciding that particular practices or actions tended to monopoly or were unfair (or, as economists would say, destructive) competition, and requiring them to be discontinued. This is the principle which eventually, in 1912, Roosevelt advocated, and which the Clayton Acts, passed two years afterward, substantially if not in a perfect form, carry out.

"America," says the most enlightening economist since Adam Smith, Alfred Marshall, "has developed the scientific application of economic doctrines to many practical problems, with great energy and thoroughness. More perhaps than any other country she has learned that general propositions in regard to either competition or monopoly are full of snares. . . . Consequently she is now engaged in leading the world in the very difficult task of restraining such methods of competition as are aimed at narrowing the basis of competition." This stage was not reached till five years after Roosevelt left office, but it is evidently the outcome of the fight which he fought.

The fight involved much bitterness, and so far only one side of the story has been told. Roosevelt never professed any admiration for the Sherman Act, which struck blindly at combination as such, with little regard to whether its results were good or bad. But public opinion had relieved itself by putting this law on the statute book, and then the Courts had made it a dead letter. Perhaps it is not unfair to say that to a once prevalent school of American political thinking this seemed a very satisfactory state of affairs. To Roosevelt it would have seemed a breach of plain duty to let the matter stay there — much as if, when Police Commissioner of New York, he had left the Sunday Closing Act, good or bad, remain unenforced.

It was important to know if the Sherman Act was really invalid. If it was, then for the same reason any better Act would have been so; if it was not, law was law. In the former case, as he told Congress in his first message, a Constitutional Amendment was needed to give the requisite powers of legislation; but immediately a case came up on which the matter could be tested. The Northern Securities Company was a probably beneficial combination of different railways, honestly carried out by one of the best of railway men on the strength of the decision in the Knight case; but it was against the Sherman Act. Roosevelt consulted his Attorney-General, Mr. Knox, and that able lawyer advised him in effect that the Supreme Court had been wrong in the Knight case and would probably find ways of deciding a new case differently. Roosevelt immediately announced his intention to bring action. Wild astonishment and indignation were aroused. The Administration won their case, and thereupon Roosevelt had action brought in every known case that arose of infringement of the Sherman Act. He was called on once to give his approval to the buying up of one concern by another in a manner intended for no other purpose than to stop a panic (which it did); but gladly and promptly as he consented, he did not do so till it was proved to him that there was no transgression of the Sherman Act involved.

From such a beginning it is obvious how hot a controversy would surround Roosevelt's career. The greatest of modern financial magnates asked him privately whether he was going to be hostile to him — as if hostility or friendship to any man was the governing motive of an Executive enforcing the law. That gentleman's state of mind and Roosevelt's amused incomprehension of it, taken together, explain the whole of his fight with the Great Business world.

It is the sort of arrogant remark which on general principles I do not think an Englishman should make, but, on reading Roosevelt's plain record, I feel that even the moderate criticism made upon his principal activities by wise and high-minded Americans shows blindness to what he clearly saw. What good came of all this fighting? To that question I think the answer has already been found by looking a little beyond his time.

It is asked, first, why harry at all a harmless body like the Northern Securities Corporation? And secondly, — since, when the big drum was beaten against him, he beat a much bigger drum in answer, — was it not an evil influence on the working class that he should talk so much of "malefactors of great wealth" and the rest of it? But, as to the first of these questions, what ought he to have done? If the Knight decision was to stand, unaltered either by the Supreme Court or by Constitutional Amendment, we can all see now, as Roosevelt saw then, that the Federal legislature was in a position of perilous impotence. If it needed courage to raise the question, yet surely it was a President's obvious duty. And when, by the practical reversal of that decision it proved that a possibly laudable combination was unlawful, it would surely be foolish to suggest that the President should not enforce the law against it. Unenforced laws are of most pernicious example anyway, and in this case there would have lain in the mouth of every perversely intelligent poor man the suggestion, with a terrible amount of truth in it, that any illegality was allowed if there was enough money at the back of it.

And this answers the further question as to his alleged inflammatory language. Labor, unless it is very different in America and in England, did not need Roosevelt to tell it that there can be malefactors of great wealth; but it very much needed him to tell it that the established order does not exist to secure them. He never suggested that all rich men or all great corporations were malefactors; on the contrary, the reader to-day of his collected speeches grows weary with his insistence, up to the utmost bounds of permissible platitude, that it is not so. Nor did he say that no poor men or labor organizations were malefactors; he hit them with all his might. And be it remembered that "malefactors of great wealth" was not an excessive term as a description of the more advanced type of unscrupulous persons contemplated by Roosevelt. That "very perfect, gentle knight," Henry Higginson, deploring his friend Theodore's inexperience, protested that the great business men whom he had dealt with in his own long business career were the most honorable men and the most useful to the community that he knew. This was doubtless true. But it was also true, for example, that a certain extremely able manufacturing company was convicted for "causing its agents to injure internal parts of rival machines when in actual use." And facts like this last get much talked about, except perhaps in the world of good and steady-going business men.

Said Roosevelt: "There are good and bad men of all nationalities, creeds and colors; and if this world of ours is ever to become what we hope some day it may become, it must be by the general recognition that the man's heart and soul, the man's worth and action, determine his standing.

I should be sorry to lose the Presidency, but I should be a hundredfold more sorry to gain it by failing to try, in every way in my power, to put a stop to lynching and to brutality and wrong of any kind; or by failing on the one hand, to make the very wealthiest and most powerful men in the country obey the law and handle their property (so far as it is in my power to make them) in the public interest, or by failing on the other hand, to make the laboring men in their turn obey the law and realize that envy is as evil a thing as arrogance, and that crimes of violence and riot shall be as sternly punished as crimes of greed and cunning." These sentiments are simple enough; but as compared with brilliant championship of one section or another, one half-truth or its opposite, unflagging and undaunted action upon these simple principles is so rare that it is hardly recognized as a merit when it occurs.

Roosevelt's fighting courage, when he was brought up against excesses on the part of labor organizations, need not be illustrated. Nor are many words necessary now upon that extraordinary exercise of watchful waiting, firmness, and diplomatic tact by which, when a long-continued coal strike threatened to become a national calamity, he succeeded in getting the dispute settled, quietly preparing in reserve his — fortunately needless — measures for seizing and working the mines. It was the year before Mr. Mundella in England induced Lord Rosebery, the Foreign Secretary, to play an equally successful part as conciliator in a kind of dispute in which such unexpected interventions might be very useful so long as they were rare. In America Roosevelt's action, helped by Hanna and encouraged by Cleveland, seems incidentally to have brought public opinion a step forward in recognizing that labor combinations, after all, exist for the protection of very real human rights.

It should be mentioned here that before he went out of office Roosevelt had a great share in the passing of the first effective Act in the United States for securing purity of food and drugs, and of the first measure involving the principle of employers' liability — both of course limited in their scope by the Federal Constitution.

In a very different direction, too, he saw the need of a bold departure from traditional policy. The alienation of public land by the Government had been a sound proceeding so far as it resulted in the creation of a great multitude of small farming freeholders. It was a very different matter when it began to result in the rapid using up of the nation's

timber supplies for private gain, — with the added
consequence of possible injury to the climate, —
the making presents to lucky individuals of mineral
wealth still belonging to the whole people, and the
falling into private ownership of water supplies
upon whose use thereafter for irrigation the fertility of large regions would depend. Enthusiasts
for the conservation of national resources had met
with his ready friendship before his Presidency,
and he worked with unremitting zeal in this cause,
from his entry into office up to the end, when he
was endeavoring — for his care of the public good
was not limited within narrow bounds of patriotism
— to procure international discussion of world-wide
questions of this kind. Frauds in the administration
of public land were vigorously checked (at the cost
of sending a Senator to jail); vast tracts of unde-
veloped wealth were set aside for the public profit;
an efficient forest-service was organized; desert
tracts were made fertile by vast irrigation-works;
sanctuaries were reserved for beautiful wild crea-
tures threatened with extinction. The high degree
of imagination which this splendid public service
demanded is unhappily illustrated by the persistent
petty opposition which it encountered.

With like imagination, he later seized upon the
fact that, with all the fine work that was already

being done by government for the technical advancement of agriculture, the life of the farming people themselves was depressed by many causes which the intelligent good-will of the community might remedy, and his appointment in 1908 of the Country Life Commission demands this slight allusion as an instance, among many, of his alert and wide-ranging sympathy.

"And who is my neighbor?" Roosevelt was one of the men who have never needed to ask themselves this question. In the normal course of administration Roosevelt was able to take some care of the Indians, whom, by the way, in an extraordinarily pathetic dying interview, Senator Quay — that great target for the reproaches of the reformers — bequeathed to his special charge. In the far larger and harder problem that concerns the Negro, perhaps with him (as with Lincoln after he had killed slavery) the example of a rare right-feeling was the one service that he could render. Englishmen cannot throw much light on this vaguely menacing problem or judge of the progress made in it. Yet a traveled Englishman is apt to have dealt with men of every possible color, and certainly must appreciate keenly that matter which sets a limit to the kindly — often extremely kindly — intercourse of the Southerner with the Black. Perhaps it should be confessed that the greatest shock which Roosevelt ever gave his English admirers was when, having invited Mr. Booker Washington to meet his wife and family at luncheon, and having set the South in a blaze by so doing, he failed to repeat his offense. But cowardice cannot be suggested in his case; he became sincerely convinced that the sensation, so astonishing to him, which he had thus aroused, was hurtful to the Negro. The matter is but one of the illustrations which he gave of a simple principle, surely incontrovertible (I am not saying that no Englishmen need to learn it), that the racial inferiority of a people, however marked, is no reason — but the contrary — for failure to give fair play to those who individually rise above the general level, or for failure to meet every man, irrespective of class or race, unaffectedly on his merits as a man.

To this slight sketch of a career in office comparable, in its record of solid achievement, to that of any great Minister for a hundred years past (say, for example, to that of Gladstone in his first Ministry), one thing must be added. It is evident that Roosevelt set his mark, in heightened capacity and devotion more conscientious and unselfish, on every branch of the service under him, naval, military, or civil, with which he had any close contact. He himself took especial pride in the testimony of a first-rate witness, Lord Bryce, who declared that in his intimate studies of government in many countries he had "never seen a more eager, high-minded, and efficient set of public servants than the men doing the work of the American Government" under Roosevelt. It is characteristic that this so especially pleased him. The quality which creates good subordinates is a quality mainly of the heart.

VI

THE INHERITED FOREIGN POLICY

ALIKE in his triumphant career as President and in the somewhat tragic course of his after-life, Roosevelt's distinction as a great Liberal at home was eclipsed by the part which he played in international affairs. That part was in its main effects greatly beneficent, while he was in power. But events followed in presence of which, whatever he might do as a father and as a citizen, his public action, still conspicuous, could only be that of a critic — some would say of a prophet. And those events were the greatest of his own or of a long preceding time. So, strangely enough, the very definite deeds of this very practical person interest us to-day far less than the principles for which he may be supposed to have stood, or rather the temper which from first to last he breathed. There was something in that temper which was faulty, there was also much that was inspiring. I make no apology here for lingering, as I shall do, over affairs which arose before he became President, and in which he was at the most a subordinate actor, though they enlisted his sympathies very keenly.

His Presidency began shortly after the commence-

ment of a new period, in which the once iso-
lated United States found that their interests —
though to an extent which even yet an outsider
should not judge hastily — were overlapping those
of neighbors across the Atlantic and the Pacific.
There was a rather mysterious little alarm concerning, in the first instance, Venezuela. It also
was becoming obvious by now that questions
about Asiatic labor would be a difficulty — perhaps
a menace one day — to them, as also to most of the
nations of the British Empire. The long agony of
Cuba at their doors had drawn them into a war
with Spain, which left them in possession of
Spanish colonies. There was further a movement —
evil in its very inception, whoever set it going
— for the portioning-out of China among other
Powers. To this America could not be indifferent,
and the matter was complicated by the Boxer
rising and the grave peril of all the Legations,
including the American, besieged in Peking. Thus
American public opinion was compelled, and has
been so more or less ever since, to envisage from
its fresh point of view questions of policy and of
principle which, through the existence of the
British Empire and of British trade, had long been
recurrent causes of controversy in England, and to
which (among us) newly awakened sympathy

with the peoples of the Dominions overseas had
added zest. Here at any rate it was the fashion then
to obscure such discussion by fallacious catchwords, such as "Imperialism," whether used as a
term of pride or of reproach, and by general maxims
to which the complex and shifting conditions of
this world, with its actual needs and duties, do not
adapt themselves. Nor does it seem to have been
less so in America. In all other great countries —
it should never be forgotten — the presence, constantly felt by every man and woman, of possibly
dangerous neighbors, gives a different cast to cur-
rent phrases and ideas.

What has been called the Expansion of Europe —
the long but intermittent process, actuated sometimes by direct pressure of population but more
often by the fear of exclusion from a market, and
resulting in the annexation by strong Powers of
uncivilized or weakly governed countries — had
proceeded with increasing vigor after 1870; and,
more recently, the passing away of Bismarck and
his policy had added Germany to the list of claim-
ants for territory overseas. Let it be granted at
once that the collective proceedings of the European
Powers in this respect presented at this time an
unedifying spectacle, and that none of them stood
above reproach. No Englishman, whatever his

preconceptions, could seriously study the history of the British Empire without upon the whole being stirred to deep gratitude and pride. But the elder among us recall incidents of that time of which we are not proud. Let it also be granted that the action of America, when McKinley was President and John Hay Secretary of State, was on the balance most highly creditable — conspicuously so in some parts of that business of China, which does not further concern our story.

But, this once said without reserve, there is a comment which I think should be added quite frankly upon the tone of American discussion of foreign affairs. Of the empires which have arisen out of the expansion of Europe, that which the original thirteen States set themselves from the first to win is the most considerable and by far the most profitable materially: so much so that the motive for further expansion was long ago completely suspended. If an outside critic with anything short of the friendliest feelings were to examine the history of its expansion, its treatment of its two subject races, the claims which it has staked out for its future influence, the customary temper of its diplomatic action, — with a few marked intervals when exceptional men have had charge, — and so on, he might find many aston-

ishingly unpleasant things to say. Yet grave and
representative American writers seem serenely convinced of an altogether superior virtue prevailing
in their country; and when a sound principle is
enunciated and followed by America, — for instance, that the Filipinos should be governed with
an unswerving view to their own welfare, as many
millions of the weak subjects of other Powers have
been governed for generations, — American youth
are solemnly taught to regard it as a new and
American invention. It would of course be as
absurd to resent this attitude as it is absurd to
adopt it; yet it is a bar to any wholesome influence
which America might exercise on men's minds
elsewhere, and hides from European eyes some
merits justly to be attributed to that country. And
this self-approving tendency, with which no doubt
the Englishmen of a day not long ago could simi-
larly be charged, seems in serious respects to falsify
some American standards. It may be to some extent a bygone evil, or it may not; but it certainly
seems to have been a common tendency, at the time
of which I write, to treat the example which an
exemplary country had set to its own self in the
past as a sufficient guide for all future action; to be
relatively uncritical of what followed along the
track of past national practice; and when needs

and duties arose which an earlier generation could
not have foreseen, to avoid facing them rather
than run the risk of straying into the ways of the
wicked Old World. From this demoralizing taint
of national self-satisfaction the manlier patriotism
of Roosevelt became more and more free.

The historical books which he wrote as a young
man are indeed flavored with that quality which
the greatest and most peace-loving of living American historians euphemistically calls "robust Americanism." Speaking, for example, of the boundary
disputes of 1846, he ignores the then infant nation
of Canada, and advocates the cherishing of an international quarrel till a convenient moment, in a
way which is cynical unless it is childlike. Again,
he must have heard of Napoleon, and it is hard to
understand how a man could make a special study
of the war of 1812 without betraying any sympathy one way or the other in that great world-
contest in which America then elected to take a
part.

American critics, who might not agree with me
in these last two points, would yet say that in
his Presidency he showed an aggressive disposition
and a certain unsensitiveness to other people's possible rights. It would be rash to say that this is
quite an unfounded censure, and I shall take some

pains to examine its insufficient foundation, but
it most certainly ignores the points which a just
criticism of him would put first.

In his maturity he was a man who loved the
thought of his country's greatness — greatness in
the largest sense. His imagination was profoundly
impressed with the elements of strife then present
(as most surely they were) in the world. He was
anxious for his country's security. Believing that
country to be honest, he thought it good for the
world that it should be strong. He thought precisely the same in regard to any truly civilized
State. He saw political and moral danger in any
tendency to think peace rather than righteousness
the final goal. Lastly, which is a somewhat different matter, his mind dwelt lovingly upon those
manly and — no less — those womanly qualities
sometimes more conspicuous in poor and struggling
than in wealthy and secure peoples, which are the
stay of family life, of the civic patriotism which
grows out of it, and of any patriotism toward the
larger human family which may grow out of that.
Deeply did he distrust any ideas of progress which
are founded in disparagement of older moralities.
This is a summary of what will be found pervading
all that he tried to teach. But it may be added
that his disposition was to go for any purpose

which he set for himself by the straightest and shortest road.

We must be clear first as to the general principles of the policy which he had defended in the Presidential campaign and to which he was now in a sense the heir. It follows from what has been said that he was a great upholder of the Monroe Doctrine; but it also follows that he did not share that sense of entire aloofness from Europe and Asia which to many minds seemed involved in that doctrine.

Perhaps an Englishman can best understand this principle — not very appropriately called a doctrine — by the analogy, once used by Senator Lodge, of the foreign policy of the British Government of India. British India together with the Native States stands in a position of relative security while their present neighbors remain as they are. That security would be disturbed and a great burden thrown upon India by the advance of any foreign Power which was likely to have conquering ambitions, into much nearer neighborhood with India. And in a lesser degree the rise of anarchy or of an aggressive despotism in a Native State or an existing neighboring State would have the same result. Against such dangers the Home Government and the Indian Government have exercised and pre-

sumably will exercise a ceaseless watchfulness.
Whether that watchfulness has always been wise
in detail, or has occasionally become rather slack,
and occasionally again nervously forcible, is a fair
question. But in broad principle there is no question either about the legitimate interest of our
governments in this matter or about their high
responsibility in it to the peoples of India and to
civilization.

Out of the necessarily indefinite British policy so
described, certain also indefinite responsibilities to
distant countries arise; but there is here no fit subject at present for any sort of express agreement or
"regional understanding" (to borrow the phrase
adopted in the late Peace Conference with reference
to the Monroe Doctrine). An intelligent foreigner,
say in France, would certainly, unless he himself
entertained conquering ambitions, say that the
whole business had better be left to the good sense
and good conscience, not infallible but still pretty
active, of that also curiously indefinable thing, the
British Empire. Its responsibility to its own citizens
must remain for the present unimpaired.

To the present critic from outside — who would
resent the term "foreigner" in this connection —
the Monroe Doctrine would seem to bear a very
closely similar aspect. In Monroe's time it was of

serious concern to the future security of the then
young America that Spain should not recover, by
the help of all the other autocratic Powers, a great
military empire in South and Central America.
Incidentally the policy of Canning lay the same
way, and the British Navy then — and with a brief
interval ever since — sustained the Monroe Doctrine as Monroe's Secretary of State meant it should
do. Unquestionably the interest of the United
States was that of civilization. At a later day the
same two interests were alike opposed to the
scheme of Napoleon III to set up the unfortunate
Maximilian in Mexico.

Later still the same interests coincided. In 1912
the following dialogue took place between an
Englishman and a Prussian sea-captain: —

"What we English do not understand is whether
you are building a fleet to sail to Paris or Moscow."

"I can quite understand you. What we really
feel is not that we want to attack you, but that
some day we shall want to expand somewhere and
shall somehow find the British navy in the way."

"Where do you want to expand?"

"Oh, say Brazil."

This illustrates at once the good sense of Roosevelt's interest in Venezuela, and of his interest in
the American Navy. And it justifies — not neces-

sarily every magniloquent statement of the famous Doctrine but the keeping of it in active life, and the keeping of it duly unlimited. It is an effective instrument of civilization, and the good sense and good conscience of the strongest Power in the Western world, and the growing amity between that Power and other American nations — of which, by the way, the second largest among the British Commonwealth of Nations is one — contribute more to the peace of the world than would any likely arrangement which weakened the Doctrine. Whatever imaginations must be permitted to Americans as to the actions of mere European countries in parallel cases, no European should allow himself to imagine, for example, that the American people will conquer Mexico unless the Mexicans really compel them to do so. The utmost abuse that could come of the Doctrine would be, say, that some conceivable Secretary of State — of the lesser sort, which seems sometimes to occur — should score an advantage in the way of concessions for an American oil-company, whose gain would leave its countrymen cold, over perhaps an English company, whose loss would cause no British tears to flow. Such a consideration, however real, is trumpery.

It is in this light that I touch upon a transaction for which I know of no quite adequate defense, but which Roosevelt was prompt to applaud: the startling procedure by which in 1895–6 Cleveland and Secretary Olney, for both of whom he had a high regard, drove Lord Salisbury to accept arbitration in a boundary dispute with Venezuela. Cleveland had some motive — which in such a man must have been high-minded — for what seemed a fantastic outrage, and Roosevelt happened to know what the motive was; but it has never been made public. If he feared that some much more sinister action than that of Great Britain dealing with the obscure frontier in No Man's Land of an existing Colony, might become hard to stave off unless he exploded as he did, that would go a long way to justify him. It may be asked: Did the actual dispute then existing involve the Monroe Doctrine at all, unless upon some really piratical interpretation of it? If there was any seeming harshness in the British Government's attitude to Venezuela, may not Roosevelt's own view later as to how to treat "pithecoid men" in Colombia have been applicable to Venezuela? Was the British objection to arbitration in this case less sound than Roosevelt's in the case of the Alaska boundary? Could not Cleveland have been sure of getting his substantial object with some exercise of elementary courtesy?

But I raise these questions to put them aside. These are secondary points after all; the main point is that the entering in of some European Power's acquisitiveness in South America was really a thing to be apprehended in those days of the great scramble for territory, and that the United States did better to bar it too hastily and too clumsily rather than too late and too half-heartedly. If it had happened, it must have been a fruitful cause of jealousy and strife and bloodshed.

Later incidents made it plain that Cleveland was Prussian only upon the surface. It should be added that English people then showed — though neither Roosevelt nor American historians since, with their references to the other troubles which may have restrained England then, seem ever to have noticed it — an instinctive conviction that war with the United States would for them, in any conceivable case, be a wicked war. Venezuela will recur to our notice very shortly, and again illustrate the fact that action which is condemned as aggressive is often that of a statesman ensuring peace.

The Monroe Doctrine is only one side of American tradition. Along with the sense that Europe should not meddle with them went the sense that they should not meddle with Europe. Both were

really part of the legacy of Washington. It was
the interest of the then young America to guard
against the most distant approach of European
aggression; it will so continue as long as such aggression is conceivable. It was, Washington said,
its interest to avoid "entangling alliances"; it is
normally the true interest of all nations at all times.
It was its interest to have as little concern as possible with external affairs except quite close to its
doors: that was a result of conditions which were
liable to change and have changed. That they have
changed very greatly is undeniable, even though it
may be absurd for agitated people in Europe to
expect official American intervention at a distance
(say in Armenia) which must make it both ignorant and impotent. American interests have crossed
the Atlantic and even more evidently crossed the
much wider Pacific. But one gathers that many
Americans long felt that the Monroe Doctrine
implied a sort of bargain: You shall not interfere
with us; we will not interfere with you. The King
of Spain, for example, shall not be a menace to us;
we will not be an offense to him.

Such a feeling, though natural and honorable,
was, if one may say so, intellectually and morally
fallacious. No government's real duties can be so
conveniently simplified; there was never any ele-

ment of bargain in the matter at all, only the eternal and ever difficult problem of right and wrong, cropping up in ever new and often unrelated practical difficulties, each to be met on its own merits.

In February 1895 there began a rebellion — not the first — in Cuba against Spain, the actual atrocity of which, and the destructive horrors resulting from the vain attempts of Spain to repress it, continued for three years to agitate American opinion. That American business interests had recently grown in Cuba does not affect the rights of the question or detract in the least from the genuineness of the sympathy of the vast majority of Americans. Opinion was divided as to the necessity and rightfulness of intervention. In February 1898 somebody blew up the American warship, Maine, in the harbor of Havana. Opinion naturally, if irrationally, precipitated itself in favor of decisive action.

Of the efforts of America, after the war, to establish a stable independent government in Cuba it would be difficult to speak too highly. Insurrectionary troubles in 1906 compelled Roosevelt to occupy the country two years; a briefer intervention occurred in 1916; but in the main the effort has prospered as well as could have been hoped.

Now Roosevelt was one of those who advocated war with Spain much earlier. Against him there are those who still think that it was right to hold off so long, and even that McKinley was wrong to go to war when he did, since it is conceivable that by longer patience with Spanish procrastination in diplomacy he might have secured Cuban independence without the formal responsibility for bloodshed. It is hardly an exaggeration to say that every important difference between Roosevelt and the critics of his own policy later may be decided on this one issue. Those who felt intense reluctance to interfering in what was (technically speaking) the internal affair of another Power, or to attacking what was (technically speaking) a friendly Power, urged considerations which are of course entitled to very great but not to exclusive weight. There is an initial presumption against intruding into a dispute between others, and an initial presumption for upholding such recognized and established rights as belong to an institution called a State; but both presumptions have their limits. The duties of an aggregate of men toward other such aggregates differ in some respects from those of individual neighbor to individual neighbor; but in some respects they are the same. Little good can be got from theoretical elaboration of rules for guidance here; the sovereign rule is that in every case the mass of individual human rights and wrongs and weals and woes should be honestly and sympathetically regarded. The claim to be made for Roosevelt as an international statesman is that he tried to do this.

The Spanish dominion was an institution which age had made decrepit, not venerable, and which decrepitude had made hardly less cruel. The insurgents who suffered and perished during three years at the doors of the Americans included many of the very pick of the great Spanish race. Their position differed only in a minute technicality from that of the remoter Spanish colonists whom the Monroe Doctrine had been promulgated to protect. Their claim differed only by being stronger from that of the American Colonies themselves when they declared their independence with a resounding appeal to human rights. They could have been helped earlier, as they were later, by an effort not really formidable. To do so would have saved much misery and death. Whoever were or were not America's neighbors, they were. The American lives eventually risked or given to save them were gladly risked and given in a cause worth living for or dying for as may happen.

It is of course no great discredit to a vast

multitude such as the American people that they did not collectively see things like this quicker. But these are the sort of things which, right or wrong, Roosevelt habitually saw. And such was Roosevelt in his Presidency and in his closing years.

Before passing from the policies which he merely inherited and completed, reference must be made to the Philippines. Of Porto Rico, which became an American dependency, nothing need be said. But the Philippine Islands were in insurrection against Spain when a turn of the war threw them into American hands, and ill chance kept them still insurgent. No American had any wish to keep them, and no American stood to gain a halfpenny out of them. It is evident that no decent course was open save either to keep and govern them for the present, or at once to start them on an independent course and to protect their independence.

Could they have then been made independent like Cuba? No man not very fully informed about the Philippines ought to venture upon an opinion. Generalities about the "white man's burden" do not settle the question, nor do the cynicisms on that subject too often quoted beyond our shores from evil-minded Englishmen who disbelieve in their own folk. British Governments with their necessarily large experience in such questions have sometimes

acted wisely either in accepting or in reject-
ing such new responsibilities, and sometimes un-
wisely in either way. Generally, as the considerations which did in fact decide them have come out
afterwards, they have been proved to have acted
uprightly. McKinley had all the attainable facts
before him. Cautious man as he was, he surely rose
to a higher level than those who would have wished
him not to "venture on untried paths." He
"walked the White House night after night until
midnight, and . . . went down on [his] knees and
prayed to Almighty God for light and guidance. . . . And one night late it came to [him] this
way: [he] did not know how it was, but it came:
that . . ." that, in short, he saw the alternatives
clear, and felt sure "that there was nothing . . .
to do but to take them all [all the islands] and to
educate the Filipinos, and uplift and civilize and
Christianize them, and by God's grace to do the
very best we could by them as our fellow men for
whom Christ also died." He guided his steps by a
less illusory light than that of common statesmen
or common theorists about imperialism and its
opposite, in the vague. He, and Roosevelt his
heir, and Mr. Taft and Mr. Root — who at Roosevelt's pressing request sacrificed their personal
ambitions, to become respectively Governor of the

Philippines and head of the department of Government concerned — in their several degrees earned the honor of all to whom the cause of the weaker races remains as dear as it was to some of our fathers.

VII

FOREIGN ACHIEVEMENTS OF THE
FIRST TERM

ROOSEVELT'S own administration of foreign affairs
affords a succession of striking incidents, not very
closely connected. Several lesser matters, highly
creditable as a rule, must be ignored here. The
triumphs of his dexterous forcefulness and swift
decision during his first term demand, unfortunately,
to be discussed at length if at all. The successes —
in reality more shining — which followed in his
second term were of a kind which can be indicated
more briefly; but the rather tedious controversies
into which I shall have first to enter exhibit fully,
without much need for comment, the strength (and
any little lurking weakness) of the man.

In December 1902 the Monroe Doctrine was put
to such a test as perhaps Cleveland or Roosevelt
foresaw in the affair of Venezuela six years earlier.
German, British, and Italian subjects had unsatis-
fied claims against the Venezuelan government
which their own governments had agreed to take
up. A German squadron, with some British ves-
sels, now began a blockade of the Venezuelan coast.
Great Britain — in Roosevelt's opinion — was half-

hearted in the matter and acted merely with the still prevailing idea of propitiating Germany. The claims in question were sound. The Venezuelan President's conduct was unsatisfactory; and Roosevelt, taking a view which hardly accords with the most extreme statements of the Monroe Doctrine, said that there would have been no objection to punitive action by European Powers, in itself. But he believed that Germany had designs of taking permanent possession of some Venezuelan harbor under cover of a long lease like that of Kiaochow and making it a fortified naval station; and his objection to this was all the stronger because it would have threatened the projected Panama Canal. Quiet diplomatic procedure through the State Department could not make Germany consent to arbitration or extract an assurance that there should be no forced lease of territory. Roosevelt then assembled in West Indian waters a battle fleet under Admiral Dewey, for manœuvres as the public supposed, but with orders — known to six persons at the outside — to be ready for instant action. At that time and at that distance the German navy would have been powerless against it. Then he personally saw the German Ambassador, explained the naval situation to him, and said that Dewey would sail, with orders to prevent any landing in

Venezuela, unless within a stated time the Germans accepted arbitration. When some days later the Ambassador paid a friendly call and had nothing to report on this matter, he was told that Dewey would now be ordered to sail a day before the date previously mentioned. Then he consulted friends who told him that Roosevelt did not "bluff." About this time Mr. Balfour, now Prime Minister, found a way of letting the world know that England would rather sympathize with American anxiety about Venezuela.

The day before Dewey was to sail, the German Emperor accepted arbitration. He solaced himself by recalling his Ambassador, and eagerly begged Roosevelt to be the arbitrator. Roosevelt's advisers, who reflected that America also had claims on Venezuela, very properly persuaded him that the Hague Tribunal should receive the practical recognition of being asked to arbitrate. Moreover, he most justly insisted that the European Naval Powers concerned should get no preference in payment over smaller European Powers with similar claims. Much complimentary intercourse now began between him and the German Emperor, who probably flattered himself ever after that they were similar characters; and the prompt vigor with which Roosevelt had coerced Germany — and in a less degree England and Italy — remained secret till after the Great War had begun. Roosevelt's own account of the matter concludes by rejoicing at the good example set by great Powers thus submitting their differences with smaller Powers to arbitration.

One of his own first acts as President had been a refusal — whether for sufficient reasons or not — to set that very example in a dispute with Canada about the boundary of Alaska; for essentially this was a dispute between the United States and a much smaller nation, whose claims, if extravagant, were not more so than those of Venezuela had been in that earlier Venezuelan controversy of 1895 in which Cleveland enforced arbitration. Great Britain, where Chamberlain was at the time bringing a new inspiration into the work of the Colonial Office, was concerned in this matter only as the trustee (in foreign affairs) of the younger nations, in a community of nations then at an early stage in the slow and delicate process of evolving relations of equal partnership. When an American writer — even Hay, if I remember — speaks in such a connection of being asked to give territory to England, he uses a phrase which conveys a seriously false suggestion. Owing to discoveries of gold, the Dominion Government of Canada had

become keenly interested in far-off Yukon. Much
annoyance began to be felt because Yukon was
deprived of near access to any but Arctic seas by the
long strip of coastal territory (running hundreds of
miles south, and overlapping British Columbia)
which an ancient treaty between Russia and Great
Britain had assigned to Alaska before the United
States bought it in 1867. The treaty no doubt had
been based upon the rights created by occupation
at the time, and there can be no doubt that the
intention was to give a substantial strip of coast to
Russia and not a string of detached headlands.
Most unfortunately, the Dominion Government
was advised to set up an interpretation of the
treaty which gave Yukon access to the sea at several
inlets. At least one greatly respected Canadian
lawyer held this view passionately; but it is not,
as I venture to think, possible to defend it.

When a Joint High Commission was appointed
to discuss a number of relatively small differences
between the two countries, Americans were inclined
to be indignant at the insistence of Canada that the
Alaskan claim should be included: it appeared to
them as if some Power, with a number of fair
subjects of difference to be adjusted with England,
should put in a fantastic claim, say, to the Orkneys,
for the purpose of trading it off in the negotiations.

The attitude of the British and Canadian repre-
sentatives while the Commission sat at Washington
in 1898–9 impressed John Hay, with all his keen
desire for friendly relations with England, very
unfavorably. He was convinced that the American
Commissioners had treated the matters in dispute
liberally; and his indignation at the way in which
they had been met was directed less against the
Canadians present than against the mere dexterous
attorneyship with which our country was represented by Herschell, the ex-Lord-Chancellor. It is
fair to add that, in the time between the Jameson
Raid and the Boer War, the British Government
generally and the Colonial Secretary in particular
may not have impressed American observers as very
tender in dealing with other people's rights.

The Commission having broken down, long fruit-
less negotiations followed, in which Great Britain
proposed arbitration. McKinley would have faced
the Senate with any reasonable proposal for a
treaty, whether for arbitration or otherwise. Hay
did not at all like to let a claim, which he felt
should never have been made by Canada, be made
subject to "the fatal tendency of all arbitrators
to compromise," and he perceived differences,
whatever they may have been, between this case
and that of Venezuela in 1895; but he said, "It

looks as if we were refusing to England what England, at our demand, granted to Venezuela." That
is what Roosevelt promptly did when he came in.
Some of his reasons can be inferred from what has
been said; and it should be said further that two
countries which speak the same language can generally settle their differences between themselves
better — as well as more quickly — than foreign
arbitrators could do it.

In 1903 there met in London a new Commission:
three Americans, two Canadians, and the Lord
Chief Justice of England (Alverstone), to whom it
fell to give the deciding vote against the Canadian
claim in the Alaskan matter. There is reason to
think that the American Commissioners insisted
very little upon some of their minor claims, though
they believed them to be in themselves sound.
When the new Commission was to meet, Roosevelt
took a step characteristically drastic and characteristically gentle in manner, to make a mis-
carriage unlikely — or in other words to prevent
any influence that might make the Lord Chief
Justice vote wrong. Avoiding the offensiveness of
any diplomatic representation, he wrote to a valued
American friend of his own and of the British
statesmen concerned, and asked to have his real
determination made known to them in friendly

conversation. It was, he said, only his "very earnest desire to get on well with England" which had made him consent to this second Commission. If it failed, he should take measures which would make arbitration quite impossible, and use the troops (which in fact he had sent to Alaska to keep order) to "run the line as we desire it, without any further regard to the attitude of England and Canada. . . . If," he said, "I paid regard to mere abstract right, that is the position that I ought to take anyhow; I have not taken it, because I wish to exhaust every effort to have the affair settled peacefully and with due regard to England's dignity." This step of his was of course not publicly known till long afterward.

The end of the whole business was entirely satisfactory: the sufficiently high-spirited British Minister to whom more particularly this pressure was applied obviously felt no offense; nor need anybody feel aggrieved about it now.

Whatever Roosevelt's real motive may have been, there is obviously something to admire in his action. Yet it may be asked, whether McKinley's attitude, as described by Hay, was not the stronger and the more dignified, and whether there was not a dangerous flaw somewhere in the man who so much applauded Cleveland in 1895 and yet was so set against arbitration a few years later. I put these questions with little doubt as to the true answer. He prided himself later on having in this instance removed "the last obstacle to absolute agreement between the two peoples," and he was certainly sincere. Now for this purpose the least risk of an arbitration which even seemed to issue in less than justice to America was a thing to be most carefully avoided, in the then prevailing temper of his own country. Of that temper in such a case Hay had lately been regretting an instance on which it is needless for me to dwell. In the subtle stroke by which Roosevelt secured that our country should do manifest justice, I believe that he worked most honestly for the cause of friendship between our peoples, which, neither more nor less than that of friendship between America and her neighbors generally, he had most deeply at heart.

I have dwelt upon this matter at such length because it seems to me a good test-case of Roosevelt's manner and spirit in his dealings, and because I happen to have a very warm affection for Canada and a passionate interest in the evolution of the British Empire. I do not want to be dogmatic, but I think it perhaps significant that I began to study this point with feelings of intense indignation against Roosevelt, and that I end with the absolute conviction that he did both a very able and a most right and friendly thing.

American comments have often been very severe upon the most conspicuous instance which he gave of swift decision in dubious circumstances. The idea of a great canal from Atlantic to Pacific is very old. It had been the subject of practical discussion since before 1850. Three routes — across the Isthmus of Panama, by way of the great lake of Nicaragua, and across part of Mexico — had been considered. No State or combination of States through whose territory it would pass could possibly afford to make it; it must be made by a foreign State or States or by a foreign company. America had obvious interests — greater even than might be supposed, since the quickest way from New York to San Francisco was: first by sea to Colon, by land across the Isthmus, and then by sea from Panama. England was interested too, as the country with the greatest sea-trade. In 1850 these Powers entered into the Clayton-Bulwer Treaty, which was intended to lead to the construction of a canal by the two together but in practical effect merely restrained America from undertaking this alone. The treaty was obscure in certain points on which close agreement was necessary. If fair treatment for everybody's shipping was assured, America could justly claim a special interest in the future canal which no European Power could have. Naturally no joint action ever was taken.

Meanwhile, the success of the Suez Canal led to the floating of a great French Company which procured a concession from the Government of Colombia for a canal from Colon to Panama. The scandals in which the enterprise came to an end in 1888 are best forgotten, if only the heroic life of Lesseps, whose last years it darkened, be remembered. The derelict undertaking of the Company, with certain assets, — of which control of the railway across the Isthmus was the chief, — passed to a new French Company, which could effect no more than to obtain from the Colombian Government the extension of the concession for some years after its original period would have lapsed.

John Hay, upon becoming Secretary of State in 1898, spent great trouble in negotiating a new treaty with England in order to get rid of the old treaty in a friendly way. But the Senate in 1900 rejected his new treaty. The gravest objection to it was that it precluded the United States from fortifying any canal which they might construct or from obtaining sovereign rights over the strips of land on each bank of it. Among the stoutest protesters against this was Roosevelt. His interest in naval matters, stimulated by the Spanish War, made a very serious point plain to him. When that war broke out, the Atlantic and Pacific fleets were separated by the length of the whole long voyage round South America. If the United States possessed a canal and could hold it by land forces, the additional strength given to their navy would be very great. If they could not so hold it, the canal might easily become an added cause of weakness in a war with naval Powers. This was a far-seeing view. It can now be seen that a combination of Germany and Japan against the United States would not have been a wildly imaginary risk to ensure against.

Recovering from great disappointment, Hay after a while approached Lord Salisbury again, found him very friendly, and eventually got a new and amended treaty ratified by the Senate a few months after Roosevelt became President. About the same time a Commission appointed by McKinley reported that the Nicaraguan route would be cheaper for a canal than the route by Panama. This judgment rested upon the fact that the new French Company was asking $109,141,500 as the purchase price of its property, whereas the Commission thought that it was worth only $40,000,000; had the price asked been this lesser sum, the Panama route would, according to the Commission, have been the cheaper. The conflict between interested and disinterested opinions favoring one route or the other became brisk in the United States.

In 1848, when California was ceded to the United States, the latter had made a treaty with Colombia, then New Granada, whereby, among other pledges of eternal friendship between the two countries, the United States acquired rights of police or military intervention in Panama to safeguard traffic across the Isthmus, and at the same time guaranteed the neutrality of Colombian territory. This guaranty was intended as against foreign invasion, not domestic insurrection, though as a matter of fact the countless interventions of America, with more or less force, on the Isthmus ever since, often requested by Colombia, had several times (once under Cleveland) taken the form of putting down insurrections by the Panama people.

The State of Panama was in international law part of the territory of Colombia, but the rights of the State, under the constitution supposed to be in force, had been violently suppressed in 1886, and without any plausible pretext of right it had become a despotically governed dependency. Moreover Panama, where there must naturally have sprung up a comparatively bustling and perhaps

unpleasantly cosmopolitan community, was shut
off from the bulk of Colombia by great mountain
masses, and was accessible from the capital, Bo-
gota, only by a fortnight's journey, including a sea
voyage. The government of Colombia was exercised — without impediment from a Congress which
never assembled — by President Maroquin. This
gentleman, having in 1898 been elected Vice-
President with the duty of filling the President's
place in his absence, proceeded two years later to
place the President in a cage and despatch him and
his cage on a bullock cart across the mountains to
a spot not far, but far enough, from the capital.
Therefore, the President being absent, the Vice-
President reigned, and, when two years afterwards
the President expired in captivity, succeeded to his
title. Such was that free Republic, sister and equal
(as some said) to the American Republic, whose
right to exact payment in respect of any possible
canal across the Isthmus constituted its most precious asset — or rather, it should perhaps be said,
the most precious asset of President Maroquin and
his friends, whose wrongs at the hands of Roosevelt are now to be considered. And such was the
relation of that Republic to the people actually
dwelling in the country to which this valuable
right of sovereignty related.

After the report of the Commission in favor of the Nicaraguan route, a bill was introduced in Congress empowering the President to construct a canal that way. Somewhat later the Commission made a further and other report, and the bill was amended in such a manner as to require the President, if it should prove possible, to make the canal across the Isthmus of Panama instead. No doubt much manœuvre and intrigue on the part of interested people was going on, and payments to persons and to party funds may have been made. But the simple and straightforward explanation of the change lies in the facts that, after the first report of the Commission the French Company decided to content itself with $40,000,000; and further, that a timely and exemplary performance on the part of Mont Pelée in the West Indies called attention to the great danger threatening any canal in a country so volcanic as Nicaragua. Roosevelt himself was strongly persuaded of the advantages of the Panama route. It goes without saying that by this time his whole heart was set upon speedily proceeding at last with so great a work so long deferred.

Hay negotiated a treaty with Maroquin's representative in Washington, who was certainly acting under instructions, and the American Senate ratified it in March 1903. It gave the Colombian Government a lump sum of $10,000,000, equal to two thirds of its then public debt, besides a rental of $250,000 to commence nine years later. It then occurred to persons in Colombia that a larger rental should be demanded, and further, that a considerable part of the price to be paid to the French Company should be paid to Colombia instead. So the Colombian Congress, which had been for five years nonexistent, met at last in June and July 1903 and duly voted the ratification of the Treaty, subject to amendments for these purposes which the Senate of the United States would certainly not accept.

It was duly felt by Americans as a comic thing that they, of all people in the world, should feel aggrieved at this failure of another country to ratify a treaty once negotiated. But there is no doubt whatsoever that the action of the Colombian Congress was a farce, produced on the stage by the executive who had negotiated the treaty. Maroquin himself, too late, offered to summon another Congress which would do as it was told. Roosevelt, who was certainly well informed, believed this business to be a scheme of a few corrupt people who would lay hold of whatever payments, larger or smaller, were made to Colombia. Not only Hay but Mr. Root entirely shared the contempt with which he resolved to treat the whole proceeding. Nothing more need be said about the Colombian Government than that, upon the failure of these demands for more money, it made a discovery that its own concession of an additional term of years to the French Company was invalid by its own laws, with the result that in 1904, when the original term would expire, it would treat all the property of the French Company as having been forfeited to Colombia.

From the moment of the breakdown of this treaty, preparations for revolution in Panama began. Four things can be said with certainty about the revolution: Active steps to promote it were taken in the United States, notably by Monsieur Bunau-Varilla, an enthusiastic French gentleman who had worked in Panama under Lesseps and now hurried over from Paris for this purpose. Signs of readiness to revolt were manifested from the very first by prominent natives of Panama, including the Governor whom Maroquin appointed and the delegates whom he summoned to the Congress. Roosevelt and Hay knew well that revolution was coming and were doubtless glad of it. Neither of them by act or word promoted it. A revolution may none the less express the prevailing desire where it happens because it has plenty of sympathizers and helpers abroad; and in this case the suggestion that the revolution was not to be treated as genuine is preposterous. What known human motive was likely to withhold most people in Panama, under the circumstances, from asserting their independence, if they could?

When reports from Panama assured Roosevelt that an outbreak was imminent, he acted upon his clear right and duty under the treaty of 1848 by sending ships to the Isthmus, with orders to prevent a landing of armed forces by either side within a certain distance of the railway. The first ship was just too late to prevent a landing of Colombian troops; but her commander succeeded among other things in keeping quiet a Colombian officer, who at one moment wanted to bombard Colon and massacre all Americans there. After some excitement, during which one Chinaman lost his life, the independence of Panama was formally proclaimed on November 4 with every sign of general acquiescence at the very least, including an unanimous vote by the municipality of the city of Panama, and the Colombian generals there were induced to sail home with their troops next day. On the sixth of November a telegraphic despatch from Hay recognized the new Government. When Colombia attempted to send troops by sea to regain

possession of the lost province, Roosevelt, with
his ships on the spot, prevented it. By November
18 Hay, working in hot haste, concluded with
Bunau-Varilla — now envoy from Panama — a new
treaty. The overtures of Colombia for undoing the
past were set aside; and the Canal, on which work
soon started under Roosevelt's close and constant
supervision, has in spite of great difficulties of more
than one kind been triumphantly accomplished.

Judgment on what thus happened has been somewhat obscured by much talk of things which did
not happen. In 1908, before the election of Mr.
Taft, certain journals gave currency to a story that
his brother and Roosevelt's brother-in-law had
received certain payments from the French Company. The implication of these stories — themselves soon disavowed and disproved — was of
course that the Government of the United States
had been corrupted. Roosevelt (very intelligibly)
felt that this was no slander of individuals but an
injurious attack upon the country itself. He conceived, or was advised, that a criminal action lay
against the offending journalists in the Federal
Courts. The Courts happily (as I conceive) held
otherwise. Meanwhile one newspaper interested
in the matter, quietly dropping the original charges,
employed an enterprising member of its staff to

inquire into the intrigues carried on in America by an agent of the French Company, the supposed connection of Roosevelt with those intrigues leading to the further suggestion that the whole story throughout was a wicked conspiracy of his against Colombia. The evidence which this good gentleman got together is to be found printed in imposing bulk in the report of a Congressional Committee. The whole mass of it is totally worthless, depending as it does upon the evidence which the said agent of the French Company unsuccessfully put forward in an arbitration in Paris for the purpose of magnifying the services which he had rendered to that Company. It should never again be referred to as an authority for anything.

Dismissing this superstructure of rubbish, what truth can we find in the severe censures upon Roosevelt which are based on the avowed facts? It is wholly creditable to American feeling that his prompt and rough handling of the Colombian Government caused a shock and long misgivings, and one's heart goes out to Senator Hoar who, after listening for a while incuriously to long explanations from the President, rose quietly and, expressing a hope that he would not be made to blush for his country, went out. Yet, with great respect, surely such men were in error. What was the moral

basis of that sovereignty of Maroquin over the
people or the land of Panama, which it is held
that Roosevelt should have treated tenderly? True,
every upsetting of any established authority among
men brings certain evils in its train, and the de-
thronement of the worst usurped power is not pure
gain. In this case the full extent of the harm was a
certain natural resentment against the United States
on the part of better republics than Colombia in
South and Central America, resentment which, if it
had no better and more lasting causes, was certain quickly to pass away.

Was Roosevelt to have hunted out supposed con-
spirators against Colombia, in America? The precedent that would have been created will not bear
thinking of. Was he to have taken any active steps
at all to keep Panama under? That too would have
been a crime. Was he, when the revolution had
happened, to allow — when he could prevent it by
a word — a bloody reconquest of Panama and a
worse repetition than ever of all its old disorders?
That would have been more in accordance with
precedent, but surely in any humane estimation of
actions and their consequences it would have been
the worst crime of all.

VIII

PEACEFUL TRIUMPHS OF THE SECOND TERM

AND now it must be briefly said how, in 1905, the
President of the United States, having done much
to enhance his country's strength and having made
his personality quietly felt in more than one land
across the seas, became one of the greatest figures
then before the world, as a devoted and most successful peacemaker. Many of us can remember
vividly how the struggle between the compact
and trained strength of Japan, and the decayed,
giant might of Russia, exerted at a vast distance,
came to a deadlock, in which national pride and
national suspiciousness withheld each country from
seeking peace, although neither could gain anything by further fighting except at a ruinous cost.
Early in this year Roosevelt, with his vividly sympathetic comprehension of the characters and situa-
tions of other countries, began anxiously to brood
on the question whether neighbors could do no
neighborly service. An Englishman, who, about
this time, had a strange intermittent talk with
him, while he simultaneously attended a Cabinet
meeting in the next room, is reported to have
brought home a quaint account of his emphatic

self-contradictory declarations, that there was nothing that could possibly be done and also that the
war must stop. It was the odd superficial token of
an intense, self-restrained watchfulness. The detailed story now before us of his intervention
cannot usefully be abridged. Its effect upon every
careful reader must be the same. I have used the
word devoted, since no weaker word can well be
applied to a man who, with overabundant work
on his hands, put, as he did, his immense industry
and resourcefulness to the severest strain which
they ever underwent, unsolicited, in a high cause,
in which rebuff and failure were most probable, and
in which success, if it was to come, would very
likely demand his trading all the credit and lustre to
others.

His task was, at first, one of incessantly feeling his way, not only with Japan and Russia,
but with France, England, and Germany. It should
be said clearly that the only noticeable help which
he found in these three neutral countries came from
the German Emperor, whose help was zealous and
valuable, and of whom his critical and humorous
estimate became tinged with real gratitude. At a
later stage when the combatant Powers showed
coy signs of a wish for peace; later still when each
was willing to negotiate, if, and if, and if; last of all

when their plenipotentiaries had met in America, and, like their armies, come to a deadlock from which only a strong arm could free them, the difficulty of the task never abated. His letters to Sir George Trevelyan, Mr. St. Loe Strachey, and others throw exceedingly pleasant lights upon the whole of this performance in diplomacy. At the close of August it ended with actual peace, just when matters had begun to seem quite hopeless. It had exacted of him throughout not only ability and courage, but unfailing patience and the sympathetic tact of a gentleman whose quality, if not always exhibited, was often almost as conspicuous as Lincoln's.

He was, too, helped here by his manly appreciation of a race so distant from us as the Japanese. The large subject of American relations with the Far East cannot here be opened up, but it may be said that the same right feeling that he showed in his attitude toward the dark races which are palpably inferior, governed him also in his various dealings with other races which, though we can never regard them from a superior standpoint, present quite as difficult a problem of human relationships. If his intervention in the Japanese struggle with Russia — in which by the way *Realpolitik* would have bidden an American statesman to let the Japanese exhaust themselves — may be dismissed so briefly, it is because in this instance nothing but frank eulogy would be in place.

What Roosevelt then did, or at least the main result of it, has long been known to the world. It is astonishing to learn since his death that, at the same time, there was in secret falling on him the chief responsibility for bringing to a peaceful issue the controversy between France and Germany about Morocco, which ended at the Algeciras Conference in the spring of 1906. The German Emperor had begged him to use his influence with France, whose "bullying," he said, could not be much longer endured, to consent to a Conference of the Powers on Morocco. The precise aims of the Emperor may be a difficult subject of speculation, but there can be little doubt that then and for some years after he genuinely desired to keep peace upon the condition that Germany got her own way, that her wishes were in all cases complied with in Europe, more particularly in France, and that outside Europe her steps toward that "world-power," of which Bismarck had resolutely set aside the idea, proceeded unhindered. France was kept perpetually alarmed and provoked. That a powerful section in Germany cherished all along a wish one day to wipe out France as a Power is, I suppose, doubted by nobody, and the moment was favorable since Russia was powerless to help France at the time.

The Algeciras Conference was one of a series of incidents which illustrated this general situation. The matter of Morocco (a country, by the way, of whose chronic lawlessness Americans had had a recent example) stood thus: France was greatly interested from the fact that she had extinguished after great provocation the sanguinary pirates who had ruled the adjacent Algeria, administered the country excellently, and incorporated it as one of the departments of France itself; indeed her interest in Morocco stood on a quite different and altogether higher level from that which any country, merely desirous to have colonial possessions or to safeguard and extend its trade, could claim. Spain was a neighboring civilized country, almost as close as Algeria. The legitimate fear of Germany at the time was that France and Spain between them, policing Morocco, would exclude German trade; beyond that confessedly lay the calculation that a special foothold of Germany in Morocco would be of future strategic value. As to the attitude of the British Government then, the most important point is that having been engaged in settling innumerable petty differences with France all over the world, which had more than once threatened to cause a senseless war, it was bound in honor (in fact by an agreement not then made public) to give diplomatic support to France in Morocco. Roosevelt half suspected that Great Britain would have welcomed war while the German Navy had not come to full strength; but of course the peril to Great Britain if Germany, when bitterly hostile to her, had conquered France would have been a standing evil, which no temporary naval triumph, however great, could have compensated.

Roosevelt was loath to take a part in the matter, for the interest of America was at the outset only that of any country, with a growing commerce, not wishful to be, by any new arrangement, excluded from Morocco or anywhere else. But he would of course do whatever might lie with him to stave off a world war, and he was anxious for the safety of France. His opinion at the moment about the attitude of Germany and, as has just been shown, of England, was not unnaturally somewhat perplexed. He was ably supported by Mr. Root, who had succeeded the dying John Hay early in 1905; and greatly helped by the wisdom and honesty of Monsieur Jusserand and Baron Speck von Sternburg, the French and German ambassadors, both dear friends of his. When he became convinced that the acceptance of the conference by France was the best way of avoiding war, he persuaded France to accept it; during the conference he further persuaded her to accept obviously just conditions in favor of nations other than herself and Spain in Morocco; and, France having readily agreed, he absolutely deterred Germany and Austria from the attempt to force upon her further concessions which would have been humiliating and were meant to open the door for future trouble. Other openings for trouble were soon found, and the Great War came eight years later; but it is clear upon the records that he more than any other man staved off the catastrophe then.

It is impossible to me not to observe with the deepest regret the comment upon this transaction of the American writer and the living historian whom I esteem most highly — one who elsewhere expresses particular pride in his country's "work towards the elevation of humanity." "It would," he writes, "I think have been better for Roosevelt . . . absolutely to refuse to interfere in a European dispute"; and there follow quotations from oddly chosen English authorities, to justify a view no less superficial than cynical of the peoples from whose struggles and agonies he would hold righteously aloof. Even so did the Priest and the Levite "pass by on the other side"; and yet Mr. Rhodes is neither a Priest nor a Levite.

It has already been mentioned that in 1906 Roosevelt had to intervene in Cuba, where certain disturbances were quieted down under the supervision at first of Mr. Taft, then Secretary of War, who was sent there. In 1905, trouble which threatened between San Domingo and its foreign creditors was quietly and permanently settled to the profit of the island as well as its creditors by sending an officer to control the customs-house. The Senate held up for a time a treaty to provide for this. The President meanwhile acted without the treaty, claiming that it was within his Constitutional powers, as not having been forbidden. Among his lesser acts it should be mentioned that very early he had shown in a most effective fashion his care for the cause of international arbitration, though he justly felt certain difficulties which made caution in it necessary for the present. Anxious that the new Hague Tribunal should be made effective, he gave the first example of having recourse to it by searching out a dispute (one with Mexico) which the United States could submit to it.

At a later period he was busy in promoting the Second Hague Convention, gracefully setting aside a suggestion that he should summon it, in order to

leave that office to the Czar of Russia, then recently
humiliated by the Japanese War; and was busy
also with certain arbitration treaties, of which the
merits and the fate need not perhaps here trouble
us. He himself sincerely felt that his most important service to peace was the voyage round the
world upon which he sent the American battle-
fleet. This great feat, as in a technical, naval sense
it was understood to have been at the time, was
actually expected by some observers to provoke
an outbreak of war with Japan. Far from having
any such result, the visits of the fleet were, in a
strange but very intelligible fashion, a cause of
friendly feeling in Japan, in Australia, and wherever
it went. Of course it made the world more aware
that in any very great struggle America counted.
Since America desired peace, that was well. It was
still more his aim to make his own people conscious
of their strength and responsibilities, and of their
neighbors.

This catalogue may fitly close by recording that,
having supported John Hay in asserting the principle of the "Open Door" — instead of rapine and
dismemberment — in China, at the close of his
Presidency he set an example to the Christian
nations by devoting to purposes for the benefit
of the Chinese people the still large unpaid bal-

ance of the indemnity due from their government.

Shortly afterwards his power was at an end. Immediately upon his election, in 1904, he had announced that he should not be a candidate again. It had been urged upon him that the usage which had hitherto debarred any President from a third term did not apply to a man who had only once been elected as President. But in his view that usage was justified chiefly by the influence which a President long in office might exercise to secure reëlection. So he debarred himself forthwith from standing again in 1908, and, when the time came, resolutely stopped the attempt to force him forward. Literally his words would have applied to any later election; but his reason for them certainly did not. It was suggested to him that he should make it clear that he would be willing to be renominated later on; but he could not wisely refer at all to things so far ahead. It was not fair that, in the events which later happened, his own "self-deny-ing ordinance," which he had amply fulfilled in the spirit, should be brought up against him as requiring a further self-effacement.

His work, conceived in no contentious temper, had only been put through by great masterfulness. He had really, and one would suppose beneficially, developed the powers inherent in his office, by doing much which seemed to him to fall naturally within the scope of the Executive, and of which there was no actual prohibition. It seems to have been sometimes feared that some President would make his office a sort of plebiscitary monarchy like that of Napoleon III, by always appealing to popular feeling to coerce the authorities constitutionally coördinate with him. The best possible critics have denied that any danger of this lay in Roosevelt. But of late he had lived in growing conflict with House and Senate, in which, till his term of office was expiring, he generally prevailed. It was, one must suppose, good that there should be a change and that the hope, originally his, of harmonious fellow-working should be restored. In any case it can seldom be good for the man, and never for the nation, that the great burden should rest on one pair of shoulders uninterruptedly for many years. But the work which he passed on accomplished was such that, looking back over forty years at least, it would be impossible to attribute to any other statesman in the world success more remarkable or more pure.

With his blustering, genial efficacy, and with manner and looks that lent themselves to caricature, — though it might most times be kindly, — with his directness that could be rasping, with his

honest catchwords, — the "square deal" and that
rather tiresome "big stick" which got associated
with the "mailed fist" and "shining armor," —
his outer man came to bulk so big under the limelight that neither the spirit within nor the real
deeds done were duly noted in his day. So at least
it was with those who watched him across the
ocean. Yet in fact he had at home given a lead
to general progress which it had sorely needed,
had done service to the poor, had advanced industrial peace, and worked for unity between races
and classes. And the warm blood, the love of fact,
the alert sympathies, which had helped him in this,
had carried his services beyond his native shores.
He had made his country safer and stronger, and
had involved it in no foreign entanglement, even
as he himself had never diluted his cherished
"Americanism" with any partiality for any one
country abroad; but he had built up the respect in
which America was held; and, steering the difficult
middle way between quixotic or meddlesome adventure and callous unhelpfulness, he had labored
truly for the cause which he defined as "the peace
of righteousness." He had groped a little and very
cautiously toward some new world-order which he
knew to be far away, but he had actively engen-
dered its prerequisite and its purpose — the spirit of

friendship. It is ill to praise a famous man to the
disparagement of the unseen hundreds who have
worked beside him, but, before that power ended
of which there could be no return, he had done a
man's part for the secure prosperity of America
and for the other and indefinable thing which can
make countries, great or small, illustrious.

IX

MANY ADVENTURES

ROOSEVELT, who, if he had an innocent taste for the limelight, did not take himself so seriously as his work, boasted chiefly about his Presidency that no man before had ever enjoyed himself in that office so much. And the happiness — and attendant sorrows — of a man who never "shrinks from the joy of life or the duty of life" were all but sure to be his still in whatever way they came. Twice again, during the strangely varied adventures of the ten years remaining to him, his prowess was fully tried in high political enterprise. Power was never again in his hands, nor did his later efforts meet with immediate success and general applause. Yet in the apparent failure — twice repeated — of his later public life he may well be thought to have consummated the work of his triumphant prime.

Barely a fortnight after the inauguration of Mr. Taft, the ex-President had cleared out of the way, sailing, with his second son, Mr. Kermit Roosevelt, and other naturalists, for East Africa, upon a mission to collect specimens for the Smithsonian Institution in Washington. If there seems to be the

least incongruity in this somewhat abrupt change
of employment, let it be remembered that Roosevelt was now, at last, entering upon the very work
which he had vainly aspired to find when he was
a student. And, during the eight exacting years
past, neither the full use of his physical endowments,
nor the delicate and intense delight in nature, nor
the high-hearted zest in comradeship with rougher
men on their own ground, had ever been allowed
to rust. For part of the voyage out it was his good
fortune to have as shipmate Mr. Selous, the gentlest
and mightiest of hunters. Landing at Mombasa,
before the end of April 1909, he worked his way by
the railway, with long excursions right and left,
to the Great Lakes, and then down by the White
Nile to Khartum, where Mrs. Roosevelt met him
in March 1910. The natural-history work, the toil
of the journey, the demand for cool daring in
tackling more dangerous game than any other land
has to offer — all these were very real. His versa-
tile vitality let him add to all this the writing (in
the evenings of exhausting days) and the punctual
dispatch, chapter by chapter, of the travel book
which he had promised to his publisher. And all
the way he studied "The Pigskin Library," that
amazing selection of sixty volumes, suitably bound

for such a journey,[1] for which he had begged when
his sister wanted to give him "a real present,"
and of which the list, ranging from Keats to Gregorovius, may be read and pondered in her book.

From Khartum he went to Cairo.

In that year's journey he had passed through
almost every degree of barbarism and civilization,
and witnessed in different forms and at different
stages the work which Christian churches and
Christian governments (when such they are) can
do in strange lands. He could take just measure
— and being a real historian who had seen some
wild scenes, had long done so — of the cynicism
and sentimentalism which lust for violent dominion, and the cynicism and sentimentalism which
deride or defame real duties done on the confines
where a trading civilization perforce encounters savagery or effete order. The quiet breed of English
men of action met him, trusted him, and told him
their difficulties. Whatever relapse may or may not
have happened under a system overstrained and
depleted of man-power by the war, an almost
unexampled work had been done when the Egyp-
tians as individuals were made free by Lord Cromer;

---

[1] " I almost always had some volume with me, either in my saddle pocket
or in the cartridge box. . . . The books were stained with blood, sweat,
gun-oil, dust, and ashes; ordinary bindings either vanished or became loath-
some; whereas pigskin merely grew to look as a well-used saddle looks
— T. R."

and in 1910 the aspiration, thus made possible, for
the freeing of a political Egypt was showing itself
in crude and dangerous forms. Roosevelt knew
that he was taking his life into his hands when
he told the inflamed Mohammedan students of
Cairo that anarchy and murder were not their
road to freedom. He was, to some extent, taking
his reputation in his hands when, later, he told
the normally slack, governing masses of England
that they must discharge their responsibilities far
away with a firmer hand. He was giving voice
to the unregarded views of his friends, the Englishmen far from home along the Nile, the fellows
of the men who had worked under him in the new
dependencies of America. He justly drew no distinction between British work on the confines of
civilization and the work, so far as it came within
his vision, of French administrators in Northern
Africa. And his real care was for "the cause of
the missionaries, of the native Christians, and of
the advanced and enlightened Mohammedans in
Egypt," and for "the Egyptian people of the
future," whose hope was then being placed in
jeopardy.

From Egypt he would have gone home had not
Lord Curzon, as Chancellor of Oxford, already
engaged him to give the "Romanes Lecture" of

1910. The honor bestowed on him by the Nobel
Prize Committee in Christiania drew him also to
Norway, which, by the measure with which he
measured human things, must be reckoned beside
the really great countries. Then the courteous visit
which he had to pay to one monarch set up a curious competition for like compliments. So the
naturalist's African expedition was followed by a
wandering of no less vivid interest through almost
every European country between Russia and Spain,
and almost every court. The tale of all this is to be
found in the private letter, perhaps the longest
extant, which Sir George Trevelyan exacted from
him as a record of their talk in Trevelyan's Warwickshire home. As to the courts — being an ex-
President, he was the only man brought up like
the rest of us who has ever mixed quite on that
footing with the strange class apart, not without
its charm and real dignity, nor shut out from public usefulness when it chose, which the then numerous princes of Central Europe constituted. His
letter contains a strangely interesting memorial of
that vanished order, and of potentates now dead
or fallen — the aged Emperor of Austria, victim
and author of much calamity, and the German
Emperor, whose ever surprising and foundationless
character he read perhaps better than anyone else,

and with equitable kindness. He also met men of higher eminence; made friends with Dr. Nansen; saw gladly from Count Apponyi that, in Hungary at least, a zealous Catholic can be a Christian Liberal; discovered no less gladly what was new to him, the solid strength of French men of affairs and men of thought, with their "unique, attractive qualities," making the best of an unhappy system arising from "the combination of the French national character and the English Parliamentary system."

While he received, he did his best to give. Hungarians rejoiced to meet for the first time a foreign visitor who knew all about the Arpád Dynasty and the Golden Bull; and it may safely be guessed that his Parisian audience at the Sorbonne appreciated the direct and homely counsels and the racy illustrations of his address to them, better than his slightly superfine critics in America supposed. His keen glance took stock pretty rapidly of the distinctive features of the popular movement in different countries. (Of Russia — unvisited — he had already prophesied that the Revolution when it came would make the red of the French Revolution look pale.) Everywhere he was happy enough, even when he had a taste of the ways of the Vatican, save only that in Prussia he was aware of a want of human kindliness in the civil welcome accorded him, and keenly sensitive of coming evil. I have indicated already that he was not in the least drawn either to indiscriminate admiration of things English, or to any idea of an exclusive political friendship with England. The true state of his international sympathies at this time is thus expressed: "Germany has the arrogance of a very strong power, as yet almost untouched by that feeble aspiration towards international equity which one or two other strong powers, notably England and America, do at least begin to feel." Words of more exact justice could hardly have been chosen.

Among the lesser of its unhappy consequences, the death of Edward VII had the effect of turning Roosevelt's visit to England too much into an affair of state pageantry and public exhibition — for President Taft made him his representative at the funeral. Perhaps he enjoyed being constantly on parade, with William II as a twin stage-figure; doubtless he enjoyed the moment, if it is true, that the latter potentate, having craved an audience with him, was granted precisely twenty minutes because Roosevelt had an appointment with Mrs. Humphry Ward. But perhaps the glare of the footlights was never quite the thing for his complexion. He met or made true friends in abun-

dance; and when Dr. Goudy at Oxford compared
Lincoln and him, "quorum alter servitudinem,
alter corruptionem vicit," he spoke the thoughts,
if not the language, of the man in the street; but
the man in the street and Roosevelt had a bad
chance of getting better acquainted. It may be,
perhaps, that when a man utters such thoughts as
the occasion demands very simply, very loud, and
with immense emphasis, he creates a quite illusory
sense of platitude; but, at any rate, kindly and
unaffected men at Oxford spoke of his Romanes
Lecture there in unappreciative terms, which they
would alter if they read it again now and considered their own lectures — though it is doubtful
whether that particular kind of discourse ever can
be really good. But that was a little thing. His
speech at the Guildhall about Egypt, to which I
have already referred, was the brave, wise, dignified
speech of an honest friend — deserving, if it be
calmly considered now, his friend Mr. Kipling's
judgment that it was "from certain points of view
the biggest thing he had ever done." It is a jarring
recollection that it was treated far and wide and
has since been remembered as an impertinence, for
of course it was quoted everywhere while the
Foreign Secretary's manful espousal of his cause
next day went unnoticed; and, considering how

English writers from Dickens downwards have favored America with their admonitions, I do not enjoy recording the fact. It should be known how far it was from impertinence. Roosevelt would not have yielded to suggestions made in Egypt that he should so speak. With real hesitation he yielded to the strong persuasion of some of the very foremost English statesmen; and obtained the full approval of the responsible Minister concerned with Egypt, before he said what could hardly have been better said, if it was to be said, and what was inspired by real courage and the fullest spirit of neighborly goodwill.

But the treasured and memorable hours of his time in England were the intimate hours with the folk who knew him best. There was that visit to Warwickshire which was to cause that enormous letter. There were Lord and Lady Lee with many a recollection to share with him; and many others whose names recall the truth that the great test of the man who happens to have traveled is the friendships that he has made abroad. Above all there was that June day's walk, whereof he and his guide, Lord Grey, have both written with loving hands, through Hampshire water-meadows and woodlands and by the incomparable clear stream of the Itchen, while his eye noted every bird, and

Grey could demonstrate Wordsworth's truth to nature, and his keen ear caught notes new to him but told him the family connections of the singer, and he gave, as Shakespeare it would seem did too, a due primacy amongst songsters to

> The ouzel-cock so black of hue
> With orange-tawny bill.

On June 18, 1910, the guns of ships and forts, the civic dignitaries at the landing-stage, and crowds innumerable in every street through which he passed, gave him such a welcome back to New York as had never before been the lot of an American citizen returning home. It was, he knew, a genuine tribute to one who had achieved a position in his own country seldom accorded to any man in any country. But a renewed demonstration next day, by a crowd suddenly collected, threw him into unusual dejection. There was an ungenuine, hysterical quality about it which set him brooding upon the crowd-mind, and gave him a presentiment, never perhaps quite fulfilled, of the unpopularity awaiting him. He had, as became him, already refused a huge salary offered to him in the business world, and accepted a much smaller one on the editorial staff of the *Outlook*. He was not exactly attracted to politics, but, as he said, "the rôle of sage had no attractions for him"; there were special causes, such as conservation of national resources and, above all, industrial reform, which he wanted to serve; and he speedily announced that he was "ready and eager to serve" in terms which no schemer after place would have used. As President he had proved his great powers and gained great experience; and he came back with powers refreshed and with widened experience. He was only fifty-two, and, to use a simile of his own, which was to become cruelly hackneyed, "as strong as a bull moose." He had always lived a life of errant, high adventure. Thus far a succession of very definite tasks had come his way. Was his next enterprise undertaken unadvisedly, or through rash ambition, or at the call of a duty more painful but quite as clear? An Englishman may handle the question ill, but I had better state decidedly the irresistible impressions made upon me.

From the day, before the end of that June when Governor Hughes, the great statesman now well known to the world, pressed the reluctant ex-President into active service, in a good cause, in his own New York State, to the day in February 1912, when seven other Governors pressed him to compete with Mr. Taft for renomination to the Presidency, — "not considering his personal interests but the

interests of the people at large," telling him that
"if he were to decline he would show himself
unresponsive to a plain public duty," — Roosevelt, with his record and known convictions, could
not with honor have acted substantially otherwise
than as he did. Already when reformers in New
York State had gone further than Mr. Hughes, and
begged him to do for them a peculiarly thankless
chore, he had said that he would not for one moment think of hesitating about answering the call
from men who were fighting for decent government
and wanted his assistance. He could hesitate as
little to lend his plain, emphatic speaking, upon repeated calls from men thus fighting, far and wide
over the country. And when the seven Governors
peremptorily summoned him, the appeal of such
calls to him had grown stronger. His thoughts are
on record. He felt sadly that all his old friends
would be against him; acknowledged calmly that
his conduct towards his successor would be blamed;
faced the probability of defeat; was deaf to considerations about his own future. "The most
important questions to-day are the humanitarian
and economic problems," and, as to these, in various ways the will of the people was constantly
being thwarted; such were the actual influences to
which senators and other legislators owed their

places, that popular representative government did not exist in America. When his friends answered him "that the public ought to be reined in and disciplined instead of being encouraged to be more lawless and self-willed," they unconsciously proved the full need of such a revival as he desired. "I wish," he said further, "to draw into one dominant stream all the intelligent and patriotic elements, in order to prepare against the social upheaval which will otherwise overwhelm us." "But," said Judge Grant to him, "the situation is complex, I suppose? You would like to be President?" "You are right," he answered, "it is complex. I like power; but I care nothing to be President as President. I am interested in these ideas of mine, and want to carry them through, and feel that I am the one to carry them through."

The next morning, February 26, 1912, his decision to oppose Mr. Taft was made public.

He was accepting an invidious part. Moreover, in the fight now beginning, he showed what some of those who loved him best imputed to him, a certain "ruthlessness." But it was fired by no petty malice and it issued in no lingering rancor; it was just the Berserker's entire determination that the antagonist present to him should go down. His was no selfish ambition, and he erred on the generous side, if he did err.

President Taft had been a dear friend, and was Roosevelt's own choice for his successor. I shall not dwell upon any point in which the President may not have fulfilled Roosevelt's expectations — not even upon the dismissal from the Chairmanship of the Conservation Board, by one of the new Cabinet, of Roosevelt's close companion, Mr. Pinchot. No minor or personal matter counted much. A new political situation had arisen with Roosevelt's departure, and he and his successor would in any case have viewed it differently. Roosevelt as President had ended in constant strife, in which he was generally master, with a powerful section of his party, ranging from conservatives of stainless honor, through an intermediate crowd of mere "items," to the dirty gang who liked intrigue and loved plunder. They controlled the Machine, and controlled on the whole both branches of Congress. From the moment that Roosevelt's successor was elected, they had, good and bad together, been reinvigorated. Meantime, among the rank and file of the party, a widespread, clamative, and boldly experimental spirit of reform had been gathering force for some years, and had made striking new departures in State legislation. In Congress too a group of Republicans, for the most part much

younger than Roosevelt and unknown when he
became President, had since 1908 been doing battle
with the established powers, and — coöperating
upon occasion with the Democrats — had won
notable victories. The reforming spirit tended to
favor some proposals which the most liberal statesmen might eye critically. The history of the time
has never, I believe, been written from the point of
view of the then President; but the present Chief
Justice of the United States is known on both sides
of the water, and it need not be explained that he
was not really, as Progressive eloquence a little
later might suggest, the Beast of Revelation. All
that now matters is that he did not regard the "old
gang" with that horrified alarm or the young "insurgents" with that sympathy, which were Roosevelt's deepest political feelings.

What young blood among the Republicans generally desired may be best judged from the rather
vast programme of National and State legislation
which it was very soon to put forward under
Roosevelt. This included a number of proposals to
secure to voters the real choice of those whom they
elected, and to the people the real control of legislation and administration. The outcome of most
of these proposals may be found in that vigorous
product, all but the last, of Bryce's long and

undefeated life, *Modern Democracies*. They were, anyway, straightforward and promising attempts to
deal with instantly pressing evils. Roosevelt himself
would have added a proposal that judicial decisions
upon Constitutional questions should be subject to
reversal by a popular vote. This was the outcome
of judicial decisions frustrating beneficial legislation, of which an instance while he was in the New
York Assembly has been mentioned, and fresh
instances had recently happened. An English lay-
man who has studied our judges' decisions in Trades-
Union cases of that time may sympathize a little
with his distrust of the courts; but this point is an
instance of a temper in his policy which might
well have provoked Mr. Taft. The programme included further the principle, already mentioned, of
control of great corporations by an executive commission, and that, which Mr. Taft himself favored,
of a standing expert body for the revision of the
tariff. There were proposals, too, very welcome
to Roosevelt, for helping the rural population in
ways which suggest the counsel of his friend Sir
Horace Plunkett. Not to attempt exhaustive treatment of so broad a scheme of policy, let it be briefly
and emphatically said that the rest of it largely
consisted in proposals of factory and social legislation, which to the average English Tory of the

time would have seemed overdue by many years.

Roosevelt came back from Europe, having taken note of the force and direction of the social movement in foreign countries, and with revived keenness to observe the like at home. His own earlier experience and his appreciation of the different elements out of which the composite American nation is ever making itself made him quite exceptionally awake to the actualities of life among the laboring mass in great cities. He must have learned lately, if he did not know long before, that in legislation for their needs every highly industrial and every progressive country of Europe was far ahead of America at that time. Men and women really working for social good had always stirred his sympathy. The "lunatic fringe" of the Progressive throng, freely as he denounced it, did not scare him. For all his genial, romping abuse of cranks he had a lurking kindness for them — save when they let their malady take a homicidal or an obscene turn. Their abundance only made him the more anxious that visions of progress should not be the monopoly of such Socialists as are blind to the community's need of vigorously directed industry, and blind to the primary moral needs of the individual man and woman. Then too, the driving-power of the Progressive movement came largely from Western people of that sort to whose fresh outlook and clean, vigorous instincts his own mind was sensitively responsive. If, besides cheer and bold leadership, such a movement needed also to be steadied and controlled, was there anybody to do it better than he? In one way or another he was bound to respond to the call of men, generally younger and always less experienced than himself, with whom he, a statesman getting elderly, could not hope to be always quite in touch, but in whose ears it was he that had first sounded the trumpet.

When the Republican Convention met in June, the controllers of the Machine had been given a long start, and had been contending for dear life. There seems to be no way of denying that the process of electing delegates to that Convention had revealed a decided preference for Roosevelt among the rank and file of Republicans, or that sharp practice went to the constituting of that Convention in a manner which ensured a majority for President Taft. The secession of Roosevelt's friends before the actual nomination, their holding of a new, Progressive Convention, which nominated Roosevelt, and his acceptance in a clear, sensible speech, — even if the closing phrase, "We stand at Armageddon and we battle for the Lord," was a trifle ecstatic, — all this cannot be called in question. The genuine choice of Blaine by misguided Republicans, to which Roosevelt had bowed, had not been an analogous case. The truth of his allegation that representative government was being turned into a mockery had been flagrantly demonstrated, and, having once said that he would accept nomination, it was plain duty now to take up such a challenge.

A brisk interchange of fighting speeches between him and the successor whom he now wished to replace soon followed, and was considerably distasteful to ordinary quiet folk. It ended with a speech delivered by Roosevelt when, on his way to make it, a crazy fellow had shot him in the chest, "as a warning that men must not try to have more than two terms as President." He refused to go to hospital till he had made that speech, with the bullet in him. "It was nothing. When I stretched out my arms, it made me gasp a little, but that was all"; but the enthusiasts, who after his speech would shake hands with him, did try his temper a bit. Replying to a question in a letter from Lord Grey, he wrote, "I can answer with absolute certainty. Your nerve would not have been affected in the least. You would have made the speech as a matter of course. Modern civilization is undoubtedly somewhat soft, and the average political orator, or party leader, the average broker, or banker, or factory-owner, at least when he is past middle-age, is apt to be soft — I mean both mentally and physically; and such a man accepts being shot as an unheard-of calamity and feels very sorry for himself, and thinks only of himself and not of the work on which he is engaged. . . . But a good soldier or sailor, or a deep-sea fisherman, or railway man, or cow-boy, or lumber-jack, or miner, would normally act as I acted without thinking anything about it." The speech slightly aggravated the wound and the bullet was never extracted; but he recovered quickly.

Meanwhile the Democratic candidate had been presented with a victory. The American people had inflicted a severe rebuff on Mr. Taft, and (it seems) soon began — here lies the fundamental difference of temper between the derided King Demos and most monarchs — to regard him with a special kind of favor. Some years later, at the height of the Great War, the two chief antagonists met by chance in a hotel. What passed may be guessed from Roosevelt's exclamation to a friend after it: "I was never so happy in my life. It was splendid of Taft." The Progressive party did not survive long. Roosevelt himself, in 1914, reflected that it had had little real coherence. Younger Progressives have said that it perished because the mighty issues raised by the Great War overshadowed its cause. However that may be, it impressed its main principles upon the nation before it died.

That being so, can one now regret what Roosevelt did? He incurred the reproach of sacrificing, to his personal ambition, the ties of party allegiance and of friendship to the high-minded statesman whom he himself had made his successor; and thereby he shook his own authority with the people at large. It is certain that he did this with his eyes open, knowing that he was injuring his own selfish interests, valuing as a condition of his future influence that very confidence in his disinterestedness which he was in part sacrificing, but judging upon the whole that loyalty to the causes which he had made his own required him to take this course at this crisis. Friends, who at the time thought his judgment most mistaken, were conscious none the less of his singular moral elevation. Whether his judgment was mistaken depends upon this further question: In his Presidency he had striven mightily to make America a Liberal country — one of those in which alert interest in social questions is deemed essential to sound statesmanship; and the work which he began has gone forward. Would it have gone forward, if in 1912 he had walked in the paths of prudence? An Englishman can only answer this with diffidence. But, I may be permitted to say, I trust that, if I had been an American, I should have been an item in the Progressive crowd which followed him.

As was fitting, he turned not very long after to his second line of interest in life, and went again upon a naturalist's travel — this time in South America. Even that most manly of rich men's indulgences, great-game shooting, was no mere play with him. This was the travel of the earnest naturalist, geographer, and social observer. Nor was his a rich man's indulgence at all. It was made to pay its way, like St. Paul's travels, by unremitting work at his craft as a writer — work of which no one who has not tried it during rough travel can guess the severity. It began with lectures which he had been invited to give in Brazil, Uruguay, the Argentine, and Chile; seemingly these republics cared little about the "rape of Panama." The Brazilian government suggested to him the exploration of the River of Doubt, of which the course was unknown, and which they renamed the River Theodore when he and his comrades had traced it fifteen hundred miles to its confluence with the chief tributary of the Amazon.

Every English boy who knows his Kingsley has

sometimes longed to travel amid the overpowering
luxuriance of the forests of South America, with all
their hidden terrors, and along its giant streams.
To me there is delight in a travel book like Roosevelt's about this journey, though there would
be no delight in my abridgment of it. But Mr.
Kermit Roosevelt has told for him what he himself
could not — the tale of his comradeship, of his sickness and dire suffering, of his courage and invin-
cible unselfishness; and a son who was a worthy
comrade to a father who was a comrade to his sons
could tell the tale with grace and authority. "Sick
as he was, he gave no one any trouble. He would
walk slowly over the portages (where till the
sickness came he had worked with the youngest),
resting every little while, and when the fever
was not too severe, we would, when we reached
the farther end with the canoes, find him sitting
propped against a tree, reading a volume of Gib-
bon, or perhaps the *Oxford Book of Verse*. There
was one particularly black night. The fever was
high and father was out of his head. The scene is
vivid before me. The black rushing river with
the great trees towering high above along the bank;
the sodden earth under foot; for a few moments
the stars would be shining, and then the sky would
cloud over and the rain would fall in torrents,

shutting out sky and trees and river. Father first began with poetry. Over and over again he repeated, 'In Xanadu did Kubla Khan a stately pleasure-dome decree,' then he started talking at random, but gradually he centred down to the question of supplies, which was, of course, occupying everyone's mind. Part of the time he knew that I was there, and he would then ask me if I thought Cherrie had had enough to eat to keep going. Then he would forget my presence and keep saying to himself: 'I can't work now, so I don't need much food, but he and Cherrie have worked all day with the canoes, they must have part of mine.'"

Such he was even in delirium. He was of the spiritual company of Captain Oates, and the comrades who watched him guessed the resolve that he had formed. If he could no longer drag himself forward, he would no longer be a burden on that party in sore peril, or a consumer of their nigh depleted stores. He would slip away into the woods and die.

He returned home in May 1914, bearing within him, it is likely, the seeds of mortal sickness, and found the Progressive policy being largely carried into effect by the skillful hand of President Woodrow Wilson.

X

THE GREAT WAR AND THE END

GREATER events now followed than any with which we have so far dealt. Roosevelt was qualified to have played a signal and a noble part in them. The part which, in fact, he had to play was all too little. As a public man, nothing was allowed to him except to reiterate warnings and protests which, whatever their ultimate effect, were generally unheeded at the moment and were often enough derided as if they had been the railings of jealousy. He came to accept the lonely task of a sort of prophet as the most useful thing left for him to do.

This was the crowning trial of his individual life. It shall be regarded here mainly under that aspect, and I refrain from the attempt to judge whether his country's actual contribution to the common cause of justice in the world could have been made at all without his warning voice. But it is necessary to say something of the policy of the President whose part in relation to the Great War and to the Little Peace was momentous, and of whom Roosevelt became, while his life lasted, the principal critic. Fair understanding of two eminent men is seldom really helped by the habit of drawing close comparisons between them. But so strong an association of ideas links Roosevelt's name with that of a later and yet more famous President, that I should be sailing under false colors if I did not expressly dissent from that estimate of Mr. Wilson which, at least till certain recent disclosures, has most frequently been expressed by Englishmen. In my eyes his singular and powerful figure appears an evil figure, which it may be right to pity but cannot be right to admire. The tendency, which has been common in England at least, to single out the name of one who has so acted, as symbolical of wide vision and high aims, is surely a tendency that must vitiate and enfeeble our appreciation of goodness.

But while it is an obligation of candor to avow the point of view from which I write, it would be out of place to defend it here. Any judgment which we can now form upon Mr. Wilson's policy must regard it as a connected whole and must largely depend on things which had not happened or which were not publicly known when Roosevelt died. A few simple and scarcely controversial remarks, which may be compatible with a different view from my own, will be preface enough to the story of Roosevelt's last struggle, involving as it did an opposition to Mr. Wilson which, if outspoken and often somewhat contemptuous, was neither unremitting nor intemperate.

The President's attitude of neutrality even in thought, at the beginning of the war, is well known; and it will be recognized now that he maintained his unconcern toward the original merits of this great conflict till continued neutrality became no longer possible for any American Administration. It received its most pointed expression in the phrase "peace without victory," as late as January 1917. It is needless to discuss here what amount of vigor and efficiency his Administration showed when once at war, for it will be conceded that this was at least fair matter of discussion at the time. One minor point, however, must be recalled in this connection because it specially affected Roosevelt and might easily have aroused in him greater hostility than it did. A proposal was early made to send forthwith to France a force of American soldiers already trained, with Roosevelt, not in chief command, but as one among the subordinate commanders. In view of the moral effect which this must have produced, it was strongly urged on the President by Monsieur Clemenceau in a letter and by Marshal Joffre in an interview; but it was rejected upon alleged military grounds.

From the moment that he became involved in

the war, the President's commanding oratory
gave his statements of war aims a vast audience in
Europe no less than at home, and in January 1918
he began to deal publicly with the terms upon which
peace could be made. As to his great speeches of
that year, it would be equally impossible now to
deny their merit as rhetorical expressions of the
general ideas of many thoughtful minds, or the need
for careful scrutiny of them in detail if they are
to be treated as anything more. Only one broad
observation need here be made upon them. They
exhibit the identity of the Mr. Wilson who was
earlier indifferent to the war with the Mr. Wilson who later gave to the League of Nations what
some would call the greatest service and others the
greatest disservice. Their strength lay in the
welcome formulation of a spirit among the Allies
which was unrevengeful and willing to look far
ahead. Their principal weakness lay in this, that
the instant rights and wrongs and the burning needs
of the moment somewhat receded into the back-
ground, while premature attention was focused on
what was not yet ripe for practical discussion. It
remains to be recalled that, as the year wore to a
close, Mr. Wilson showed himself resolved on having, so far as America was concerned, a free hand
to procure such a peace as he thought right. Just

before the Armistice he had appealed to the electors
to return a Congress of men who, whatever their
attitude in the war, would support him personally.
Having failed in this, he avoided all consultation
with representative Americans whose opinion might
differ from his own, and, in disregard of a good deal
of protest, proceeded himself to Europe as, for
practical purposes, the sole and uncontrolled representative of his country. Further we need not follow
him, for Roosevelt died just when Mr. Wilson was
about to go to Paris, where he was to share with
Mr. Lloyd George the chief responsibility which
can be attributed to individuals for the existing
settlement of Europe.

Roosevelt had returned from Brazil about ten
weeks before the War began. He was but barely
recovering from a terrible illness suffered amid
privation and overexertion. By the end of August
he was able to undertake speeches, though physi-
cians seem to have advised that he must retire from
public life. He certainly did not retire and he spared
himself very little; but he seems henceforth to have
been conscious, as never before, of a limit to the
vital force now left in him, and when he schemed
to go to France in 1917 it was with the full conviction that active service meant death to him.

Apart from the War which soon came, the political situation to which he returned was a disagreeable one for him and one for which he was specially responsible.   He found ardent Progressives eagerly looking for him, but there was nothing encouraging in the condition of the party or the attitude of the country towards it. He gave some rousing addresses to gatherings of Progressives in Pennsylvania, in August, and helped in a vain attempt to elect a candidate of the party to the Governorship of New York State, though wisely refusing to be that candidate. But in November he candidly confessed to friends the failure of the whole attempt to found a new party. It had been based too much on lofty general principles to appeal to the average man; it had had too many extravagant people in its ranks, and its existence offended against a deep-seated habit which made people regard it as natural to have two parties only, each of which could be punished when it went wrong by voting for the other. Incidentally he began now to give up the idea, which he had started, of the referendum on judicial decisions; the courts had of late, he thought, returned to the wise tendency, once exhibited by Marshall, to construe the Constitution in favor, where possible, of giving authorities the necessary power for their necessary purposes. Some have attributed this salutary change chiefly to his influence.

He was very happy in himself, as he declared in
an intimate letter, but his position was not one in
which people could easily believe him to be so.
In becoming the Progressive leader he had accepted
a call to show the way between supporting the
"sordid machine-crowd" and joining "a set of reformers who came dangerously near the mark of
lunacy"; and now he had to disappoint men who
had been with him in 1912, and whom he heartily
respected, but who could not see, as he did, that the
hope of support had disappeared from them. On the
other hand, there were more men than ever whom
he had offended, and they rejoiced to think him
politically dead.

One advantage he thought he had in his iso-
lated position; he could preach sound doctrines
about capital and labor without any longer being
identified with wild people. Otherwise he was
no longer a force, and it would be a great mistake for him — he said in November, when the
elections had shown that the Progressive party was
defunct — to take any part in politics at the
moment. "As things are now," he wrote at this
period, "I am entirely out of touch with the
American people." Again: "When it is evident
that a leader's day is past, the one service that he
can render is to step aside and leave the ground clear
for the development of a successor." Again: "It

would be foolish for me or my friends to blink the
fact that, as things are now, my advocacy of a man
or a policy is in all probability a detriment and not
an aid. The people as a whole are heartily tired of
me and of my views."

If this caution was necessary in all that he might
say politically, it applied from the first with special
force to whatever he might say about the War.
And the subject of the War must have been very
difficult to any American statesman. When a great
struggle breaks out in which well-informed and
right-thinking people must sympathize strongly
with one side, it does not in the least follow that
they should wish their own country to intervene
immediately; the danger of such a general rule of
conduct, if any country were likely to adopt it, is
obvious. There is no doubt what Roosevelt's
feeling was from the first. The situation of mutual
jealousy and suspiciousness, between Germany and
each of the three Great Powers then arrayed against
her, was one of which he had been able to watch the
development at an earlier stage; but he was not,
like the President, in a position to know that the
German rulers had for some time been determined
to force on a war. All his inborn prejudices, and
his very great liking for many Germans (especially
in America) no less than for his French and English

friends, helped him to regard the first few steps in the process by which the outbreak came on more or less fatalistically, as if the conflict had been bound to come one way or another. But a point had quickly arisen on which he could not feel neutrally for a moment, and which made what had gone before immaterial. This was the violation of Belgian neutrality.

He explained in October to the British Ambassador, Spring-Rice, that, if he had been President in the last days of July, he would have claimed the right of America as one of the signatories of the Hague Treaties to have Belgian neutrality respected, and would have ranged the United States alongside of England on that issue; he believed that the people would have been with him. It is conceivable that this would have stopped the War. Nobody who has watched his record can doubt for a moment that he would have acted so, and no one not obsessed with a distrust of the American people can doubt much that they would have followed him.

That opportunity was missed, and Mr. Wilson is not the only statesman who would have missed it. Still the opportunities for some protest — a real protest which would at some point have been made good in action — went on, beginning with the breaches of the Hague Convention which recurred every day in Belgium. The President might fairly have been presumed then to have some honorable object in view, and even his famous words about neutrality might claim at first to be read as an avoidance of unnecessary offensiveness before he acted — such avoidance as Roosevelt was ever inculcating in international conduct.

Roosevelt had at that time no strong feeling of antagonism toward Mr. Wilson; he had for some time thought him "an adroit man, a good speaker and writer, with a certain amount of ability of just the kind requisite to his party," only "not a man of great intensity of principle or conviction"; but that was all. And Roosevelt knew better than most men how likely it was at such a crisis that a statesman in power should be holding his hand, owing to knowledge which he could not at the moment disclose, and which no one outside could guess. It was exactly the sort of temporary crisis — never lasting for long — at which a responsible statesman in opposition is bound by a rule which irresponsible critics never observe; he must not embarrass the Administration by any hasty utterance such as may quite likely make more difficult the very line of conduct which it is intended to encourage. Probably there was nothing yet for him to say — least of all could he, as some people have

since suggested, have encouraged an unfortunate
deputation of Belgians to rely upon action by
America which he could not promise.

It is, however, a useful rule that when one has
nothing to say, one should be careful to say it.
Roosevelt — unfortunately, as things turned out —
published an article in the *Outlook*, which could be
taken later as an expression of neutrality of thought
as hopeless as Mr. Wilson's own but less straightforward. It might be read now as just one of those
pieces of bad writing to which a facile writer is
prone, which are the more thoroughly bad because
every paragraph taken singly is rather good; it is
even comically reminiscent of the writer's own
criticisms later of Mr. Wilson's "weasel-worded"
phrases — numerous passages in it simply suck the
life-blood out of the passages coming before or after them. We know now that it was inspired by the
hope that some protest on behalf of international
law was coming from the President. How could a
patriotic man, with Roosevelt's knowledge and no
more, have failed to cherish that hope? Knowing
now his intention, we can spell out his meaning.
He could not, for an undeniable reason, have said
outright what he thought should be done. But he
could, and he did, indicate quite plainly the definite
cause of quarrel on the part of America which justi-

fied some intervention, going on as he did to insist that if there was any intervention it should open courteously but be seriously meant, and to insist that, whatever happened, America must be prepared for war which might come on her. The article is incidentally interesting because it contains the hope, expressed cautiously but more sanguinely than he later expressed it, that there might come out of the War, ultimately, a league of the civilized nations for righteousness.

The abundance of stuff in it which his friends thereafter remembered with painful feelings, and which has the air of apology for German aggression, really served a purpose. Roosevelt, it must be remembered, had a special sympathy for the German element in America not yet in the mass committed to a German and un-American attitude. If the stand for international right was taken, the balanced and sympathetic tone of this article would have made it serviceable as an appeal to them. As it was, it merely served to give some plausibility to very ungenerous criticism of him later.

From this point on, the course which he took is plain and simple, nor need consideration of what was bound to be chiefly negative criticism of bygone acts or omissions by others detain us very long. Here as elsewhere I have considered at length

action of his upon which, at first, I should have
thought those who blamed him right, and have
found myself forced to the conclusion that the
blame comes to nothing when his actual situation
is really envisaged.

The first opportunities for protest soon passed,
and as they passed, and the President's real attitude
became plain, all reason for reticence passed too.
He "kept silent," as he wrote to Mr. Kipling, "as
long as he thought there was any chance that Wilson
was really developing a worthy policy." And
indeed, but for those addresses to Progressives in
August 1914, one of which was the first strong
appeal made to Americans to put their country
permanently in a position of being able to defend
itself, he kept silent in public a little longer. The
sense that he was out of touch with prevailing
opinion evidently weighed upon him. In the letter
of October 3 to Spring-Rice, already cited, he says:
"I believe that if I had been President the American
people would have followed me. But whether I am
mistaken or not as regards this, I am certain that
they are now following Wilson. Only a limited
number of people could or ought to be expected to
make up their minds for themselves in a crisis like
this; and they tend, and ought to tend, to support
the President in such a crisis. It would be more than

folly for me to clamor now about what ought to be done, when it would be mere clamor and nothing more.''

But by the beginning of 1915 matters had so developed that it became well to speak, and speak again, at any risk of being unheeded or of arousing at first only opposition. It was evident now how long and terrible the War would be, and evident that America would sometime and in some way be involved. Moreover the pro-German sentiment and activity in America, the stimulation of which was the real and inevitable effect of the President's declared "impartiality," had begun to take menacing shape. On the other hand, General Leonard Wood, the soldier of first repute in America, was starting the movement by which he trained many thousands of volunteers in camps organized and supported by volunteer effort. Roosevelt then began a course of speaking and writing in which he ceaselessly insisted upon three points: the infamy perpetrated in Belgium, the need of preparation, the obligation of undivided loyalty to America on the part of every citizen of whatever origin. It is certain that with a firm mind, thenceforward to the end of his days, he accepted the odious position of the prophet who must deliver his message regardless of how much he may provoke, and of how much the

seeming effect of his testimony may be to attract
hostility to his doctrine.

Mr. Alfred Noyes allows me to publish a letter
which serves, like others already published, to show
very clearly just what he felt.

November 28, 1914

MY DEAR MR. NOYES:

I am greatly pleased with your letter and with the
poem [one published by the London *Daily News*,
appealing to America to come in]. I very sincerely
believe in peace. I hold the man, who, in a spirit
of levity or wantonness or brutality or mere fancied
self-interest, goes to war, to be an abhorrent brute.
But, as the world now is, I am convinced that peace
will only come on the same terms on which we get
it in great cities — that is, by doing everything to
cultivate justice and gentleness and fair dealing between man and man and between man and woman,
and at the same time having a court backed by
physical force, that is, backed by the police power,
to which one can appeal against the brutal, the
disorderly, the homicidal. I believe your verses
will be of benefit here; for too many of our peace
people have degenerated into the ultra-pacifist
type. None of our peace bodies, for instance, have
ventured to denounce Germany for her destruction

of Belgium, which is, on the whole, the most hid-
eous crime against peace and civilization that has
been perpetrated since the close of the Napoleonic
wars. They hold little futile peace-parades, and
send round peace postage-stamps with a dove on
them, and get up petitions for peace in the public
schools; but they do not venture for one moment to
condemn any man who has done wrong, or to do
more than raise a feeble clamor to the effect that
peace must be obtained by tame acquiescence in
wrong.

Sincerely yours,

THEODORE ROOSEVELT.

P.S. I am not anti-German; I am anti-brutality!
I should protest as quickly against wrong-doing by
England or France or Russia; and more quickly
against wrong-doing by the United States.

In May of that year there came a fresh and much
clearer call to action by the United States. It came
upon Roosevelt under very strange circumstances,
which were tending then to make him heard as
readily as of old, and which made the manner of
his response the most signal act of a life rich in
action.

In the course of the autumn Roosevelt had seen
cause to denounce the head of the Republican

organization in New York State, Mr. William Barnes, as a machine politician of the baser sort. With a temerity which greatly annoyed enemies of Roosevelt, who thought that they "had him dead and buried" politically and that he should have been left so, this gentleman brought an action for libel. The case was tried at Syracuse in the spring of 1915. The effort of the prosecution was of course to show that Roosevelt had throughout his career used the kind of dishonorable political trickery which he denounced in others. Vast quantities of his old letters were unearthed, and every passage of his career was closely investigated. For six days he underwent the most rigorous cross-examination. As to the effect of it, his own deep pleasure was that nothing passed in that trial which he would not have wished his children to hear, nor is there any doubt that that trial was fatal to any attempt that could or can be made to cast suspicion of any serious reproach upon any part of his political career.

On the afternoon of May 7 nothing remained but that the jury should be set to consider their verdict. Their finding would be upon the reputation of a man who valued his countrymen's regard, and was deeply sensitive about the lesson of purity and un-selfishness which he had sought to teach them, and which would be all undone if his practice could be thought inconsistent with what he preached. There were upon the jury two, perhaps three, men of German origin, and Germans in America were already angry with him.

That afternoon came the news of the sinking of the Lusitania. Roosevelt said nothing to his lawyers; he was not going to ask for advice which would either be such as they should not give or such as he should not take. He talked much that evening to his host; but consulted neither him nor any man; said that his course was clear; and went to bed. Shortly he was woken and called to the telephone. A New York editor told him the detailed news. "That's murder," he said. "Will I make a statement? Yes, yes. I'll make it now. Just take this." And he dictated a short, emphatic message, ending: "It seems inconceivable that we can refrain from taking action in this matter, for we owe it not only to humanity but to our own self-respect."

In the morning he saw his lawyers: "Gentlemen, I am afraid I have made the winning of this case impossible. But I cannot help it if we lose the case. There is a principle here at stake which is far more vital to the American people than my personal welfare is to me."

Now as a matter of fact the case was not lost. The German-American jurors gave an honest verdict. There was an even stranger sequel; later, when America went to war, Mr. Barnes himself was among those who begged Roosevelt to become Governor of his State; he had creditably learned and said frankly that a crisis had come when the country needed men of exceptional honesty. But of course the likelihood was great that Roosevelt's words would throw his case away. Easily could a plausible reason have been found for withholding that statement. The excuse that the President must not be embarrassed would have been unsound, because all the facts were clear and it was a question of doing or not doing the thing that was known to be right, but it was an excuse — and there were others that would have served — which would have contented most critics. A moment's honest thought will show not only how many public men but how many of our private selves would have failed under that test.

I have heard people dismiss this incident lightly because Roosevelt's mental organization was such as made his reaction to stimulus very quick. But what a life lay behind the man whose instantaneous reactions were of this self-devoted kind.

To me, I must simply say, this deed seems to rank among the "Golden Deeds," and the doer of it ranks among the men about whom laudatory rhetoric can be dispensed with.

The statement on the telephone was followed up and reiterated, and as, even then, for nearly two years more America held back or was held back, Roosevelt's voice was uttered ceaselessly, upon the simple lines already indicated, as "the voice of one crying in the wilderness." So at least it seemed to him, or rather, — for his thought on this subject was very clear and very manful, — he passed definitely into the class of those servants of humanity whose efforts are all the while producing indefinitely great results but at a cost of a steadily mounting hostility to themselves. I may pay my debt late because some one has cursed me for not paying it, but I shall pretend to myself that I am paying it for some quite different reason, and I shall be an exceptionally noble fellow if I feel much gratitude to him.

One strong view which he now developed requires a word. He was of course an ardent supporter of the proposals of Secretary Garrison and Senator Chamberlain, in 1915, for universal service — proposals which arose out of the teaching of General Wood and himself. It seems unnecessary to say much of this now, for when war is impending, the pretense of some superior virtue, in preparing the defense of one's country too late rather than too soon, can hardly be convincing even to its

own strangely numerous expounders. But Roosevelt
came during the war to regard universal service as a
sound permanent system. One who used to work
under Lord Roberts when he was advocating the
same cause in England before the War, may be for-
given for making a comment here. The proposal
was, by the way, damped down by the great War
Minister, Lord Haldane, in England because he
knew that the moment when we were changing our
system would be the moment for Germany to strike.
But the proposal seemed good to many of us then,
as it did to Roosevelt, on purely social grounds.
Military training might have been made to supply
to many poor lads some of the advantages which
richer people's sons derive from Universities, and
its effect in bringing social classes together would
in countries like America and our own be great.
But a military establishment in excess of actual
military needs cannot of course be defended because
of the by-products that might be got from it. The
felt unreality of it would be fatal to them. This is
evident enough; I refer to the matter only because
in this connection as in many others Roosevelt
evinced the keen interest which he took in all that
may tend to give to laboring men a larger life.

The Presidential election approached, that strange
election upon which an Englishman's comments

would be uncomprehending. It became plain to Roosevelt that he could not be a helpful candidate to those who were eager to run him, and to the chagrin of many of them he withdrew himself and turned to speaking for Mr. Hughes, but on lines of plain dealing with the great issue which both parties were at the moment seeking to avoid. Then suddenly America was in the War. Reference has already been made to the proposal that a division of the men already trained should go forthwith to France, with Roosevelt among the subordinate commanders; to the great moral effect which this must have had in making the fact that America, with its inexhaustible resources, was now in the war felt by Germans, by the Allies threatened with disheartenment, and last not least by the American people; to Roosevelt's own conviction that he would die if he went; and to the immortal jest of Mr. Wilson's "scientific" precision [of military science] in overruling the petition of Marshall Joffre. It must be added now that his friends regard this as the greatest disappointment which in all his life he had had to bear.

He went on undismayed with the task set him, speaking, writing constantly in the *Metropolitan* and sending off one hundred and fourteen editorials to the *Kansas City Star* in the last sixteen months of his life. That journal put them at the service of as many other papers as chose to avail themselves of its public spirit; the last was actually written the day before his death and contains his final remarks on the League of Nations.

To any one calmly reading now the volume of these republished articles, the fury which they and Roosevelt's other dying utterances provoked in many breasts and the pitying regret which they unmistakably roused in others, seem rather melancholy — not altogether strange. There are doubtless considerations of etiquette which apply to ex-Presidents, but evidently these should be waived at a sufficient crisis. There is also, possibly, a feeling that a country best shows its high resolve by conspiring to praise its rulers all the time — it is the German principle. It is a mischievous fallacy to say that honest criticism is embarrassing to an Administration; it can be so only when there is definite ground for supposing that the Administration is doing better than you know, for reasons which you do not know. There was no ground for that supposition then.

The anger of those who dropped taking the papers with those articles, or who wrote to say that Roosevelt should be "shot at dawn," comes back to this, that it is not pleasant to people beginning to make an effort to be told that they must make much greater efforts; perhaps still less pleasant, when those greater efforts are being made with some success, to have it explained, with the astounding candor which Roosevelt used toward America, how far more other people have contributed to the great result. There is nothing in all that he said which approaches that violence of controversy to which every popularly governed country is too well accustomed. Nor did the writer fail in his hearty and ungrudging welcome of the action of the President's which he could approve. Nor, outspoken as were his criticisms upon many things and many men, was the staple subject of his writing mere negative criticism of anybody at all. His persistent theme was the encouragement, in the direct and blunt language to which only he laid claim in speech or writing, of all the wholesome feeling and the honest effort then stirring. It was not of high policy only that he wrote, but of the right attitude of honest Germans toward America and of honest Americans toward them, of all that could be done for the enlisted men, of the part of the workmen in the war, of thrift among the poor, of the right influence of mothers on their sons; and if much that he said was matter for the moment only, it was sound matter. This applies more particularly to his free criticism of the

Administration; it was conspicuously honest in all cases, it was manifestly just in many; it is hard to see where it can have been other than useful.

Not to revive past controversy unduly, there was need that the war once begun should proceed more vigorously than at first; there was need to examine closely the loose phrases about the peace settlement which the President seemed to propound as exact statements of principle; there was need to make sure that the President's policy should not go back from staunch support of his allies to a lax attitude of concession to his enemies; there was need lastly to insist, if possible, that the effort to found a League of Nations should begin by the effort to make existing friendships secure, and the effort to prevent future crimes in general should begin by stopping all chance of recurrence of the actual crime still recent.

In regard to the League he failed. Upon the other points, which I instanced, surely it is most likely that the uplifting of this constant voice of warning did much to ensure that steady pressure of general American opinion upon the Administration, which prevented the danger of a great collapse from coming nearer than it actually did. But here I deliberately leave public controversy lightly touched. It was at any rate not perversely nor without cause that

Roosevelt took up his parable in the spirit of Garrison, and could have said of himself, in the words of the first number of the *Liberator:* "I will be as hard as truth and as uncompromising as justice. I will not equivocate; I will not excuse; I will not retreat a single inch; and I will be heard." Still laboring in this task, he died.

Before it was ended he and Mrs. Roosevelt had partaken in the proud sorrow of those countless fathers and mothers who in a sufficient cause gave the lives of their dearest as they would gladly have given their own — of those mothers to whom, whether their sons were taken amid the stress of action or under the hand of that fell epidemic which ravaged American training-camps, he had addressed in the articles of which I spoke words of tender comfort with the ring of truth in them. All their four sons had gone to the war. Two were wounded. Three were decorated. On July 17, 1918, he was about to address the Republicans of his State, then as often in sore straits, when the news reached him that the youngest, Quentin, the funny little boy of a few years ago whose quaint thoughts had inspired some of his most charming letters, had fallen in France in aerial combat. He made that speech as he had prepared it; then he added "to the women primarily, to the men also" whose sons were fighting, words worthy of the sorrow in which he stood, appealing for the consecration to ordinary life at home of "such fealty and idealism" as their sons were showing in the field.

In the *Metropolitan* that autumn he said: "Only those are fit to live who do not fear to die; and none are fit to die who have shrunk from the joy of life and the duty of life. Both life and death are part of the same Great Adventure. Never yet was worthy adventure worthily carried through by the man who put his own personal safety first. Never yet was a country worth living in unless its sons and daughters were of that stern stuff which bade them die for it at need; and never yet was a country worth dying for unless its sons and daughters thought of life not as something concerned only with the selfish evanescence of the individual, but as a link in the great chain of creation and causation, so that each person is seen in his true relation as an essential part of the whole, whose life must be made to serve the larger and continuing life of the whole." He was told that he had never written so well before, and answered, "Ah, that was Quentin."

Very shortly after writing this he was taken to hospital for an operation. He returned to that dearly loved home, and resumed his unwearied work. "After this"—namely on January 6, 1919 — "it was noised abroad that Mr. Valiant-for-Truth was taken with a summons." So begins that great quotation with which the secretary of his Harvard classmates announced his death to the class, with which two of them have ended their books upon him, with which his old friend, Senator Lodge, adorned a noble speech, and to which I can add so little.

That little had best be very simply said. I am of course well aware of the crudity and fleeting worth of this study. But when I undertook it I made one demand — namely, that I should be amply briefed with the worst that had been said of Roosevelt. That demand has been fulfilled faithfully, and I have faithfully tried to use the material before me. I need hardly add that I have met a number of people with personal impressions, favorable or unfavorable, to give of him. I have indicated where his faults seem to me to have lain, and if I have not laid more stress upon them it is because I believe that to dwell more on these light and often laughable matters would be to draw things in false perspective. Men have fought as stoutly as he, and more wisely — seldom so consistently for the right. That is the main thing. The grosser charges that have been flung against him in no instance demand one word. Of the more intellectual and refined sort of criticism of him, I feel, to speak frankly, the prevailing inhumanity, the failure to understand those simple qualities which go to the hearts of common people, and of which the full possession is greatness, whether genius accompanies it or not.

In the affairs of nations he had been a successful pacificator; this was possible to him because he was quick in sympathy and personally capable of generous friendship. He had tried no less to be a reconciler in social and industrial strife; here too his power arose out of his ready understanding of individuals and his promptitude to recognize worth in men and women of whatever kind.

I will not again recur to political controversy. If we have much to learn from him as a statesman, the foundation of it rests on this: that he lived no restricted life of mere statecraft, any more than of mere scholarship, or mere sport, but that he took life whole, as it offered itself, and that, in like manner, he respected worth when it met him and welcomed friends as God sent them, careless of differences between nations, or between classes, between gentle and simple, between the like and the unlike to himself.

I began this book by avowing a hero-worship of long standing. I do not mean by hero-worship any disposition to found a cult of the hero, to use his name as a rallying cry for party, or to shape one's own life in any spirit of discipleship to him. There is only one honest and useful discipleship possible to men. Great men are only worthily honored if the honor we pay them provokes us, the weakest or stupidest, to stand resolutely erect. And least of all would Theodore Roosevelt be worthily admired by anyone whom the mere power of his mental and physical machinery should impress as the real wonder of his life. My own pleasure, as I have tried to trace his steps, has been the growing sense that Mr. Valiant, with his "courage and skill," his "marks and scars," bore himself as the true and gentle companion of Mr. Ready-to-Halt and of Mistress Much-afraid.

A LETTER FROM THEODORE ROOSEVELT
TO LADY DELAMERE

THE letter reproduced in facsimile on the following pages is in the possession of the Roosevelt Memorial Association, which has kindly permitted its use in this book. It is believed never to have been published before. Apart from its rare autobiographic interest, it has a history which should be related.

The recipient of this letter was the daughter of the Earl of Enniskillen, and the wife of Lord Delamere, a pioneer of colonization in British East Africa, with a large estate near Nairobi. She died in 1914.

After the sacking of a house in Ireland, in the course of the recent troubles there, a Scottish soldier, detailed some time later to the scene, found scattered on the lawn many of the effects of the family to whom the house belonged. Among other articles he came upon this letter which, with a realization that it might be worth having, he preserved. At a still later day, after his return to Scotland, he found himself in need of money and sold the letter to a dealer, in whose shop it was seen by an American, a college classmate of Roosevelt's biographer, Mr. Joseph Bucklin Bishop, whom he informed of the circumstances. Mr. Bishop called the attention of the Roosevelt Memorial Association to the letter, and the possibility of securing it. The Association promptly purchased it for its collection of manuscripts, of which the remarkable document is now a part.

O Lady; I wish I could tell his both you my kind... than I do ... Faithfully yours Theodore Roosevelt

warmest regards

SAGAMORE HILL.

Mar 9th 1911

Dear Lady Delamere,

I prized your letter. Indeed I do know that you and Delamere have the large outlook, that your own success comes second to the feeling that you have taken the lead in adding to the Empire the last province that can be added to the whiteman's part of it. He has

rendered to East-africa,
and therefore to its greater
Britain, a literally
incalculable service, I only
wish that in England
itself there was a fuller
appreciation of the service.
But it must necessarily be
that the great services to
any empire are rendered by
men who are not overmuch
heeded by those who stay
at home and who play,
not for the really great
stakes, but for primacy
where "vanity is trimmed
with lace" — to paraphrase.

I know just how you feel about
England now; there are real dangers
ahead. Yet I can not but believe
that — the self — is there (S now it;
though its greatness and its future)
depend upon its sons and
daughters who dare the Great Adventure,
and not upon those who care only
for easy pleasure and for its excitement
that is rich; nor — really (There is plenty
of excitement — that is health;) but — this
being as an excitement — (a corrosen of nothing—).

Well, whatever comes, you and Delamar have played your parts well and bravely, you have done well what was well worth doing; and I could wish nothing better to be said of those that are dearest to me.

As for me, I have never been happier than for the last four months. When I reached home I was acclaimed with a reputation that was far in excess of my deserts, and therefore over-weighted and over-weighted being reaction. On the afternoon I seem to see the afternoon

my landing, when I had
been given a greeting to
which I was not in the
least entitled, a greeting
that would have been a
trifle per-fervid if extend-
ed to a Washington or a
Lincoln under such circumstances, I told one of my
sisters that I was like
Peary at the North Pole — I
had nowhere to walk except
south. The expectations were
great, were utterly vague, utterly contradictory; I had not the
place, I had not the power or
the position to satisfy them in
the smallest degree; and yet
I did not feel at liberty

to draw off and refuse to
do what I regarded as the
plain duty of a citizen. As
for the attacks on me, the
wave of popular disappointment, I literally do not
care a rap. I am sorry
to disappoint good, foolish
people; but I am sorry
for their sake, not mine.
I was really uneasy and
concerned about the
over-praise, the over-admira-
tion and the impossible
expectations; but I do
not mind in the least
when they go to the opposite
extreme; and neither the
praise nor the blame makes

one particle of different in my career; I have worked hard; and now I have revelled in staying quietly here in my own home; I will there for whom I have worked in the world; was with my own body; and the thing with which I have associations.

Twenty years ago, even ten years ago, this would not have been so; I would have felt that it spelled failure to have me faced out of the contest while it was still my business to fight; But now I have fought; I am entirely ready to

take up any task which I ought to; but
if no task comes, why I feel I have done
enough to warrant my enjoying to rest
without— its bounting sense of having
failed to strain my best while it was
still the day of action. Will us in this
into political power comes for short, passing
than with you, but— is most victory while
it lasts; Lincoln's career was for but
eight years; Hamilton's was less; for the
continuing one of the men who reached the
summit— had careers that lasted longer—?
was even in its inability to its success.

a President has a great
chance; his position is almost
that of a king and a
prime minister rolled into one;
once he has left office he
can not do so very much;
and he is a fool if he fails
to realize it all and to be
profoundly thankful for
having had the great chance.
No President ever enjoyed
himself in the Presidency as
much as I did; and no
President after leaving the
office took as much joy in
life as I am taking.
There! See what an
egoistical outburst you
~~brought~~ on yourself!

It was fine your being able to be with your boy. Ever since you showed me his letter my heart has warmed towards the little fellow.

Lord Grey and his daughter were out here the other night, and he told me of the death of poor George Grey. I liked him much; he was a game, hard man in danger and difficulty, and yet with real kindliness and gentleness of character. He

had killed a longo, a
bull, shortly after Kermit
killed his cow and calf,
and he gave it to us to
complete the the group.
Well, lions are "bad
medicine", as we used to
say in the cow country!
Especially if hunting them
is followed up long
enough. It's a marvel
your husband survived.
I hope Alfred Pease won't
get caught; poor fellow,
he was heart-broken over
the death of his wife.

By the way, I took a
great fancy to Edward
Grey; he's a trump.

Kermit is working well at Harvard, and is enjoying himself; altho he is not quite in such touch with his fellows as if he had not made his eighteen months trip to Africa and Europe — naturally enough — and altho of course he longs for Africa now and then. We are just starting for California, to see our eldest son and his wife; he is at work there; and we shall see one of our other boys who is in Arizona, at school.

How I do hope that we shall see you here some day! I want to show you all my family; I have told them much about you and how I prize your friendship

The conclusion of the letter will be found in the margins of its first page

INDEX

INDEX

ADAMS, JOHN (PRES.), 64.
Africa, R's Travels in, 159–162.
Alaskan Boundary Dispute, 116, 128–134.
Algeciras Conference, 149, 150.
Alverstone, Lord, 131.
"Americanism," 6, 75, 110, 157, 196–198.
"Ananias Club," 84.
Apponyi, Count, 164.
Arnold, Matthew, 35.
Arthur, Chester A. (PRES.), 43.

BALFOUR, LORD, 127.
Barnes, William, 199, 201.
Belgium, 191, 192, 196.
Bimetallism, 81, 82.
Bishop, Joseph B., *Life and Times of Theodore Roosevelt*, 4; quoted, 47, 214.
Bismarck, 107.
Blaine, James G., 28, 177.
Boxer Uprising, 106.
Browning, Robert, quoted, 60.
Bryan, William Jennings, 82.
Bryce, Lord, quoted, 104; *Modern Democracies*, 173, 174.
Bunau-Varilla, Philip, 141, 143.

CANNING, GEORGE, 114.
Carnegie, Andrew, 74.
Chamberlain, George E., 202.
Chamberlain, Joseph, 128.
Chaplin, Lord, 81.
Clayton Acts, 92.
Clayton-Bulwer Treaty, 134.
Clemenceau, Georges, 185.
Cleveland, Grover (PRES.), 29, 39, 81, 100, 116, 117, 125, 128, 132, 137.
Colombia, 116, 134–145.
Conservation of national resources, R's policy on, 100, 101.
Corporations, Bureau of, 91, 92, 93.
Costello, Mike, 25.
Cromer, Lord, 161.
Cuba, in revolt against Spain, 119–122; 153.
Culture, American, at end of 19th century, 78, 79.

Curzon, Lord, 162.

DEMOCRATIC PARTY, R's opinion of, 81.
Dewey, George, 50, 126, 127.
Dickens, Charles, 167.
Doubt, River of, 180.

EDWARD VII, King of England, 165.
Egypt, R's speech at Cairo, 162; R's speech at the Guildhall, London, concerning, 162, 166, 167.

FRANCIS JOSEPH I, Emperor of Austria, 163.

GARRISON, LINDLEY M., 202.
George, Henry, 38.
George, Lloyd, 187.
Gladstone, William Ewart, 41, 42, 56, 57, 103.
Goudy, Henry, 166.
Grant, Robert, 171.
Gregorovius, 161.
Grey, Lord, 167, 177.

HAGEDORN, HERMANN, *Roosevelt in the Bad Lands*, 4, 33.
Hague Tribunal, The, 153, 154.
Haldane, Lord, 203.
Hamilton, Alexander, 64.
Hanna, Marcus A., 85–87, 100.
Harrison, Benjamin (PRES.), 39.
Hay, John, as a member of R's cabinet, 83; his attitude on the Alaskan Boundary Dispute, 130, 132, 133; Negotiation for the Panama Canal, 135–145; 89, 91, 108, 128, 151, 155.
Hayes, Rutherford B. (PRES.), 43.
Herschell, Lord, 130.
Hoar, George F., 144.
Hughes, Charles Evans, 169, 170, 204.

INTERSTATE COMMERCE COMMISSION, 92, 93.

JACKSON, ANDREW (PRES.), 81.
Joffre, Marshal, 185, 204.
Johnson, Andrew (PRES.), 77.

Jusserand, Jules, 151.

Kansas City Star, R's war editorials in, 204.
Keats, John, 161.
Kelly, Peter, 25.
Kingsley, Charles, 180.
Kipling, Rudyard, quoted, 166; 195.
"Knight Case," 90, 91, 95, 97.

LABOR, 75-77, 97-99.
Lang, Lincoln, 36.
League of Nations, 186, 205, 207.
Lee, Lord and Lady, 167.
Lesseps, Ferdinand de, 135, 141.
Lincoln, Abraham (PRES.), 6, 55, 77, 88, 102, 166.
Lodge, Henry Cabot, 39, 93, 112, 210.
Longworth, Alice (Roosevelt), 18.
Lusitania, sinking of, 200.

McKINLEY, WILLIAM (PRES.), death of, 55; 39, 40, 80, 82, 86, 108, 123, 130, 132, 136.
Macaulay, Lord, 57.
Mahan, Alfred T., 49.
Maine, U.S.S., 119.
Maroquin, Pres. (of Colombia), 138-145.
Marshall, Alfred, quoted, 93, 94.
Marshall, John, 188.
Maximilian, Ferdinand, Emperor of Mexico, 114.
Monroe Doctrine, 112-127.
Mores, Marquis de, 33.
Morocco, French and German controversy over, 149-152.
Mundella, Mr., 100.
Murray, Joseph, 20.

NANSEN, FRIDTJOF, 164.
Napoleon I, 110.
Napoleon III, 114, 156.
New York Legislature, analysis of, 21-23.
Nicholas II, Czar of Russia, 154.
Nobel Prize, awarded to R, 163.
Northern Securities Corporation, 95, 96.
Noyes, Alfred, 197.

"OPEN DOOR," 154, 155.
Outlook, R as an editor of, 168.

Oxford University, R's "Romanes Lecture" at, 162, 166.

PANAMA, State of, and Canal (see Colombia).
Philippines, 109; insurrection against Spain, 122-124.
"Pigskin Library," 160, 161.
Pinchot, Gifford, 172.
Platt, Thomas C., 53, 54.
Plunkett, Sir Horace, 174.
Porto Rico, 122.
Progressive party, its inception and its part in the Presidential election of 1912, 172-179; 182, 188, 189, 190.

QUAY, MATTHEW S., 102.

RAILWAYS, American, their place in American politics and economy, 69-71; and the Interstate Commerce Commission, 92, 93.
Republican party, its history and composition, 19, 81-83; at the time of its fight with the Progressive party, 172-177.
Rhodes, James Ford, quoted, 28, 152.
Riis, Jacob, How the Other Half Lives, 45.
Roberts, Lord, 203.
Robinson, Mrs. Douglas, a sister's record of R's life, 12.
Rockefeller, John D., 75, 90.
Roosevelt, Alice Hathaway (Lee), 18; death of, 31.
Roosevelt, Edith Kermit (Carow), 38, 160.
Roosevelt, Kermit, 159, his description of R's sickness during their South American travels, 181.
Roosevelt, Quentin, 208, 209.
Roosevelt, Theodore,
Autobiography, 4, 25; birth and ancestry, 4, 5, 7, 8; understanding of England and the English, 5, 6, 161; a Unionist, 7, 8; physical weakness in childhood, 8; eyeglasses, 9; excellence in sports, 9, 12; philosophy of sports, 9, 10, 178; as a naturalist, 10, 11, 159-161, 167, 168, 180-182; early travels, 11; letters to his children, 12; years at Harvard College, 13-17; his book on The Naval His-

tory of the War of 1812, 14; decides to enter politics, 16, 17; first marriage, 18; Republican candidate for New York Assembly, 20; in the New York Legislature, 20-28; his democracy in politics, 24, 25; his oratorical style, 26; delegate to Republican National Convention (1884), 28, 29; life in North Dakota, 30-37; loses mayoralty election in New York City (1886), 38; second marriage, 38; as a member of United States Civil Service Commission, 41-45; as President of the Police Commission of New York City, 45-50; as Assistant Secretary of the Navy, 49, 50; in the Spanish War, 50-52; as Governor of New York, 52-55; an estimate of his character, 55-61; as President of the United States, 80-158; and his Cabinet, 83, 184; and the "trusts" (Sherman Act), 88-89; and labor organizations, 99, 100; and purity of food and drugs, 100; and the public lands, 100, 101; and agriculture, 101, 102; and the Indians, and the Negroes, 102, 103; his general attitude toward foreign affairs, 110-112; and the Monroe Doctrine, 112-127; his interest in the Navy, 114; his attitude toward the Spanish War, 120-121; his action in the Venezuela affair, 125-128; his action in the Alaskan Boundary Dispute, 128-134; his opinion and action in the Colombia-Panama affair, 140-145; as a peacemaker between Russia and Japan, 146-149; as a peacemaker in the Morocco controversy between France and Germany, 149-152; his action in regard to San Domingo, 153; and the Hague Tribunal, 153, 154; and the "Open Door" in China, 154, 155; an estimate of his career as President, 155-158; his travels in Africa and Europe (1908-1910), 159-168; awarded the Nobel Prize, 163; as an editor of the *Outlook*, 168; as the Presidential candidate of the Progressive party, 169-180; his "ruthlessness," 171; is wounded, 177; his travels in South America, 180-182;

his endeavors to lead an expeditionary force to France, 185, 204; his last illness, 187, 208, 209; his opinions on the World War, 190-208; his feelings toward Woodrow Wilson, 192, 193, 195, 205, 206; tried for libel, 199-201; his support of universal military training, 202, 203; his war editorials in the *Kansas City Star*, 204-208; his son, Quentin, is killed in the war, 208, 209; his death, 208, 209, 210.

ROOT, ELIHU, as a member of R's cabinet, 83; as Secretary of War, 123; as Secretary of State, 151; 140.
Rosebery, Lord, 100.
Rough Riders, 39, 51, 52.
Russo-Japanese War, 146-149.

SALISBURY, LORD, 116, 136.
San Domingo, 153.
Selous, Frederick C., 160.
Shakespeare, William, quoted, 168.
Sherman Act, 90-95.
Smithsonian Institution, 159.
Sorbonne, R's address at the, 164.
South America, R's travels in, 180-187.
Spanish War, 50-52, 106, 119-122.
Spring-Rice, Cecil, 39, 191, 195.
Sternburg, Baron Speck von, 151.
Strachey, J. St.-Loe, 148.
Strong, William L., 39.

TAFT, WILLIAM HOWARD (PRES.), as a member of R's cabinet, 83; as Governor of the Philippines, 123; as Secretary of War, on a mission to Cuba, 153; as President, 159, 165; as a Republican candidate for the Presidency against R, and Woodrow Wilson, 169-179.
Tariff, the, R's avoidance of and opinion concerning, 89, 90.
Thayer, William Roscoe, *Theodore Roosevelt, an Intimate Biography*, 4; quoted, 14.
Tolstoi, Leo, 35.
Trevelyan, Sir George, 4, 148, 163.
"Trusts," their growth and influence on American conditions, 71-75; R's dealings with, in his Presidency, 88-99.

VENEZUELA, 106, 114, 116, 117, 125–128, 130, 131.

WALPOLE, SIR ROBERT, 86.
Ward, Mrs. Humphry, 165.
Washington, Booker T., 103.
William II, Emperor of Germany, 127, 147, 163, 164, 165.

Wilson, Woodrow (PRES.), elected to the Presidency, 178; an estimate of his character and his actions as President, 183, 187; 59, 182, 191, 192, 193, 206, 207.
Wood, Leonard, 40, 196, 202.
Wordsworth, William, 168.

Printed by McGrath-Sherrill Press, Boston
Bound by Boston Bookbinding Co., Cambridge